AF422449

Contents

GRILLED GARLIC AND HERB SHRIMP

Servings: 4 | Prep: 10m | Cooks: 5m | Total: 2h15m | Additional: 2h

NUTRITION FACTS

Calories: 336.4 | Carbohydrates: 10.2g | Protein: 37.8g | Cholesterol: 345.6mg | Sodium: 400.8mg

INGREDIENTS

- 2 teaspoons Spices, paprika
- 2 tablespoons Garlic, raw
- 2 teaspoons Italian seasoning
- 2 tablespoons Lemon juice, raw
- 1/4 cup Oil, olive, salad or cooking
- 1/2 teaspoon Spices, pepper, black
- 2 teaspoons dried basil leaves
- 2 tablespoons Sugars, brown
- 2 pounds Shrimp, fresh, raw, large (21-30)

DIRECTIONS

1. Whisk the paprika, garlic, Italian seasoning, lemon juice, olive oil, pepper, basil, and brown sugar together in a bowl until thoroughly blended. Stir in the shrimp, and toss to evenly coat with the marinade. Cover and refrigerate at least 2 hours, turning once.
2. Preheat an outdoor grill for medium-high heat. Lightly oil grill grate, and place about 4 inches from heat source.
3. Remove shrimp from marinade, drain excess, and discard marinade.
4. Place shrimp on preheated grill and cook, turning once, until opaque in the center, 5 to 6 minutes. Serve immediately.

CREAMY SHRIMP SCAMPI WITH HALF-AND-HALF

Servings: 2 | Prep: 5m | Cooks: 15m | Total: 20m

NUTRITION FACTS

Calories: 1175.1 | Carbohydrates: 106.9g | Protein: 59g | Cholesterol: 405.4mg | Sodium: 959.4mg

INGREDIENTS

- 1/2 (16 ounce) package GG Linguine Pasta Semolina-Dry-5/8"Crcl QK
- 2 teaspoons Lemon juice, raw

- 4 tablespoons Butter, with salt
- 2 cloves Garlic, raw
- 1 pound Crustaceans, shrimp, mixed species, raw
- 2 tablespoons Alcoholic beverage, wine, table, white
- 1/2 cup Cream, fluid, half and half
- 1/4 cup Cheese, parmesan, grated
- 2 tablespoons Parsley, raw

DIRECTIONS

1. Bring a large pot of lightly salted water to a boil. Cook linguine at a boil until tender yet firm to the bite, about 8 minutes.
2. While pasta cooks, melt 2 tablespoons butter in a skillet over medium heat. Add garlic and cook until fragrant and lightly browned, about 1 minute. Add shrimp and cook until tails start curling in, about 2 minutes per side. Add remaining butter, Pinot Grigio, lemon juice, half-and-half, and Parmesan cheese. Stir to incorporate.
3. Drain linguine and divide noodles between 2 bowls. Serve shrimp mixture on top and garnish with parsley.

SHRIMP MOZAMBIQUE

Servings: 6 | Prep: 10m | Cooks: 35m | Total: 45m

NUTRITION FACTS

Calories: 348.5 | Carbohydrates: 28.7g | Protein: 15.5g | Cholesterol: 155.7mg | Sodium: 3277.2mg

INGREDIENTS

- 1/2 cup Butter, with salt
- 1 large Onions, raw
- 10 cloves Garlic, raw
- 1 (12 ounce) can Alcoholic beverage, beer, regular
- 1/4 cup Alcoholic beverage, wine, table, white
- 3 (1.41 ounce) packages sazon seasoning
- 1 dash Sauce, ready-to-serve, pepper or hot
- 1 pinch Salt, table
- 1 pound Shrimp, fresh, raw, large (21-30)
- 3 cups Rice, white, long-grain, regular, cooked
- 1 tablespoon Parsley, raw

DIRECTIONS

1. Melt butter in a large skillet over medium heat. Add onion and garlic and cook until tender but not brown, about 5 minutes.
2. Stir beer, white wine, sazon, hot sauce, and salt into the skillet. Bring to a boil. Reduce heat and simmer for 15 minutes.
3. Add shrimp to the skillet and cook until pink, 3 to 4 minutes. Add rice; heat through for about 5 minutes. Stir in parsley.

SPANISH GARLIC SHRIMP (GAMBAS AL AJILLO)

Servings: 4 | Prep: 15m | Cooks: 5m | Total: 20m

NUTRITION FACTS

Calories: 227 | Carbohydrates: 2.5g | Fat: 15.1g | Protein: 18.8g | Cholesterol: 173mg | Sodium: 344mg

INGREDIENTS

- 4 cloves garlic
- 1 pound frozen large shrimp (21-25 count) - thawed, peeled, and deveined
- kosher salt to taste
- 1 teaspoon hot smoked paprika (optional)
- 1/4 cup extra-virgin olive oil
- 2 tablespoons dry sherry
- 1 tablespoon chopped Italian flat-leaf parsley

DIRECTIONS

1. Slice garlic thinly. Season shrimp with kosher salt and paprika. Mix to coat.
2. Heat garlic and oil in a skillet over medium heat. Cook until garlic starts to turn golden, about 2 minutes. Add shrimp and increase heat to high. Toss and turn shrimp with tongs until starting to curl but still undercooked, about 2 minutes. Pour in sherry. Cook, stirring continuously, until sauce comes up to a boil and shrimp is cooked through, about 1 minute more. Remove from heat. Stir in parsley with a spoon.

GRAIN BOWL WITH BLACKENED SHRIMP, AVOCADO, AND BLACK BEANS

Servings: 4 | Prep: 20m | Cooks: 50m | Total: 1h10m

NUTRITION FACTS

Calories: 695.7 | Carbohydrates: 61.8g | Protein: 32.5g | Cholesterol: 175.4mg | Sodium: 2032.1mg

INGREDIENTS

- 1 1/8 cups Water, municipal
- 1/2cup dirty rice mix
- 1 pound Crustaceans, shrimp, mixed species, raw
- 1 tablespoon Spices, chili powder
- 2 teaspoons Spices, paprika
- 1 1/2teaspoons cumin, ground
- 1 teaspoon Spices, onion powder
- 1 teaspoon Salt, table
- 1/4teaspoon Spices, pepper, black
- 2 tablespoons Oil, olive, salad or cooking
- 1 (15 ounce) can Corn, sweet, yellow, canned, whole kernel, drained solids
- 1 Peppers, sweet, red, raw; red bell pepper
- 1/4 cup Cilantro, raw
- 1 Lime juice, raw
- 1 tablespoon Oil, olive, salad or cooking
- 1 Avocados, raw, all commercial varieties
- 1/4cup Cilantro, raw
- 1/4cup Greek yogurt
- 1 clove Garlic, raw
- 3 tablespoons Oil, olive, salad or cooking
- 1/2 teaspoon Salt, table
- 1/4teaspoon Spices, pepper, black
- 1 (15 ounce) can Beans, black turtle soup, mature seeds, canned
- 1 Avocados, raw, all commercial varieties
- 1 Limes, raw

DIRECTIONS

1. Combine water and dirty rice mix in a saucepan and bring to a boil. Reduce heat to low and cover. Cook until water is absorbed, about 45 minutes. Remove from heat and let stand 5 minutes. Fluff rice with a fork and set aside until needed.

2. While rice is cooking, combine shrimp, chili powder, paprika, cumin, onion powder, salt, and black pepper in a bowl.
3. Heat oil in a medium cast iron skillet over medium-high heat. Add shrimp and cook until no longer pink, about 2 minutes per side.
4. Mix corn, red bell pepper, cilantro, lime juice, and olive oil together in a bowl to make corn salad.
5. Combine avocado, cilantro, yogurt, garlic, olive oil, salt, and black pepper in a food processor. Pulse until dressing is smooth.
6. Assemble bowls by dividing cooked rice, cooked shrimp, corn salad, black beans, and sliced avocado evenly. Drizzle with dressing and garnish with lime wedges.

SHRIMP DE JONGHE

Servings: 6 | Prep: 15m | Cooks: 25m | Total: 40m

NUTRITION FACTS

Calories: 429.1 | Carbohydrates: 12.2g | Protein: 49.3g | Cholesterol: 483.3mg | Sodium: 1213mg

INGREDIENTS

- 3 pounds Crustaceans, shrimp, mixed species, cooked, moist heat
- 2/3 cup Bread crumbs, dry, grated, plain
- 1/2 cup Fleischmann's Cooking Sherry II
- 1/4 pound Butter, with salt
- 1 large clove Garlic, raw
- 1 teaspoon Salt, table
- 1 pinch Tarragon-Whole-Dried FO
- 1 pinch Spices, marjoram, dried
- 1 teaspoon Parsley, raw

DIRECTIONS

1. Preheat the oven to 400 degrees F (200 degrees C).
2. Place shrimp in a baking dish.
3. Combine bread crumbs, sherry, butter, garlic, salt, tarragon, and marjoram in a bowl. Sprinkle mixture on top of shrimp in the baking dish. Sprinkle parsley on top.
4. Bake in the preheated oven until golden brown, about 25 minutes.

GRILLED SPICY SHRIMP TACOS

Servings: 20 | Prep: 15m | Cooks: 25m | Total: 1h40m | Additional: 1h

NUTRITION FACTS

Calories: 187 | Carbohydrates: 20.9g | Protein: 13.9g | Cholesterol: 103.7mg | Sodium: 226.1mg

INGREDIENTS

- 1 1/2cups Lime juice, raw
- 3 tablespoons Oil, olive, salad or cooking
- 2 tablespoons Spices, chili powder
- 1 teaspoon Salad dressing, mayonnaise, soybean oil, with salt
- 3 pounds Shrimp, fresh, raw, medium (31-35)
- 1/2cup Enchilada Sauce, ready-to-serve
- 1/2 (4 ounce) jar Peppers, jalapeno, canned, solids and liquids
- 5 teaspoons Honey, strained or extracted
- 3 teaspoons Lime juice, raw
- 1 pinch Salt, table
- 1/2 head Cabbage, red, raw
- 2 bunches Onions, spring or scallions (includes tops and bulb), raw
- 3 tablespoons Oil, olive, salad or cooking
- 3 tablespoons Distilled Vinegar
- 1 small bunch Cilantro, raw
- 20 (8 inch) Tortillas, ready-to-bake or -fry, corn

DIRECTIONS

1. Mix lime juice, olive oil, chili powder, and mayonnaise together in a bowl. Add shrimp and marinade for at least 1 hour.
2. Mix enchilada sauce, jalapenos, honey, lime juice, and salt together in a separate bowl for the sauce.
3. Toss cabbage with scallions, olive oil, vinegar, and cilantro in a large bowl for the slaw.
4. Heat tortillas in a frying pan over medium-high heat, about 30 seconds per side. Keep warm.
5. Preheat an outdoor grill for medium heat and lightly oil the grate.
6. Remove shrimp from marinade. Grill until opaque, about 5 minutes. Add shrimp to each tortilla; top with the sauce and slaw.

KETO SHRIMP SCAMPI

Servings: 3 | Prep: 10m | Cooks: 25m | Total: 35m

NUTRITION FACTS

Calories: 224 | Carbohydrates: 6.8g | Protein: 19g | Cholesterol: 190.7mg | Sodium: 461.4mg

INGREDIENTS

- 2 (8 ounce) packages shirataki noodles
- 1 tablespoon Oil, olive, salad or cooking
- 1 tablespoon Shallots, raw
- 2 cloves Garlic, raw
- 1/4 teaspoon dried red pepper flakes
- 12 ounces Shrimp, fresh, raw, medium (31-35)
- 1/4 teaspoon Salt, table
- 1/8 teaspoon Spices, pepper, black
- 3 tablespoons Lemon juice, raw
- 3 tablespoons Alcoholic beverage, wine, table, white
- 2 tablespoons Butter, with salt
- 1 tablespoon Parsley, raw

DIRECTIONS

1. Cover shirataki noodles with water and bring to a boil. Boil for 5 minutes. Drain.
2. Return drained noodles to the saucepan and cook over medium heat to remove any excess moisture, 5 to 6 minutes. Remove from heat and set aside.
3. Drizzle olive oil into a large skillet over medium heat. Add shallot and stir until translucent, 2 to 3 minutes. Take care not to burn. Add garlic and red pepper flakes; stir for 1 minute. Add shrimp and cook for 2 to 3 minutes per side, taking care not to overcook. Season with salt and pepper.
4. Transfer shrimp to a bowl, reserving pan drippings in the skillet. Whisk lemon juice and white wine into the skillet. Add butter and cook until fully incorporated and sauce begins to thicken slightly, 3 to 4 minutes.
5. Return shrimp to the skillet. Add noodles. Sprinkle with parsley and toss to combine.

TASTY SHRIMP TEMPURA AND SAKE DIPPING SAUCE

Servings: 4 | Prep: 20m | Cooks: 7m | Total: 2h27m | Additional: 2h

NUTRITION FACTS

Calories: 488.8 | Carbohydrates: 57.8g | Protein: 27.5g | Cholesterol: 223.8mg | Sodium: 3814mg

- 2 eaches Shallots, raw
- 1 cup Soy sauce made from soy and wheat (shoyu)
- 1/4 cup Sake (Saki) Wine (Japan)
- 1 tablespoon Hot Chili/Red Pepper Sauce
- 1 tablespoon Cilantro, raw
- 1 tablespoon Ginger root, raw
- 1 cup Rice flour, white
- 1 cup Water, municipal
- 1 Egg, yolk, raw, fresh
- 1 pound Shrimp, fresh, raw, large (21-30)
- 1/2 cup Rice flour, white
- 2 cups oil for frying

DIRECTIONS

1. Mix shallots, soy sauce, sake, hot pepper sauce, cilantro, and ginger together in a bowl; let sit, about 2 hours.
2. Mix 1 cup rice flour, seltzer water, and egg yolk together in a bowl.
3. Split shrimp down the center, cutting almost but not completely through, and open flat. Pat with paper towel to dry; dust with 1/2 cup rice flour. Dip shrimp in batter until thoroughly covered.
4. Heat oil in a deep-fryer or large saucepan to 375 degrees F (190 degrees C). Cook shrimp in small batches in oil until golden brown, about 7 minutes. Remove shrimp from oil and place on paper towel to absorb excess oil. Serves dipping sauce alongside the shrimp.

MARINATED GRILLED SHRIMP

Servings: 6 | Prep: 15m | Cooks: 6m | Total: 55m | Additional: 34m

NUTRITION FACTS

Calories: 273 | Carbohydrates: 2.8g | Protein: 31g | Cholesterol: 230mg | Sodium: 417.8mg

INGREDIENTS

- 3 cloves Garlic, raw
- 1/3 cup Oil, olive, salad or cooking
- 1/4 cup Tomato products, canned, sauce
- 2 tablespoons Regina Red Wine Vinegar-50 grain NB
- 1/2 teaspoon Salt, table
- 1/4 teaspoon Spices, pepper, red or cayenne
- 2 pounds Crustaceans, shrimp, mixed species, raw
- 6 eaches Skewers

- 2 tablespoons Basil, fresh

DIRECTIONS

1. In a large bowl, stir together the garlic, olive oil, tomato sauce, and red wine vinegar. Season with basil, salt, and cayenne pepper. Add shrimp to the bowl, and stir until evenly coated. Cover, and refrigerate for 30 minutes to 1 hour, stirring once or twice.
2. Preheat grill for medium heat. Thread shrimp onto skewers, piercing once near the tail and once near the head. Discard marinade.
3. Lightly oil grill grate. Cook shrimp on preheated grill for 2 to 3 minutes per side, or until opaque.

SZECHWAN SHRIMP

Servings: 4 | Prep: 10m | Cooks: 10m | Total: 20m

NUTRITION FACTS

Calories: 142 | Carbohydrates: 3.7g | Fat: 4.4g | Protein: 18.3g | Cholesterol: 164mg | Sodium: 500mg

INGREDIENTS

- 4 tablespoons water
- 2 tablespoons ketchup
- 1 tablespoon soy sauce
- 2 teaspoons cornstarch
- 1 teaspoon honey
- 1/2 teaspoon crushed red pepper
- 1/4 teaspoon ground ginger
- 1 tablespoon vegetable oil
- 1/4 cup sliced green onions
- 4 cloves garlic, minced
- 12 ounces cooked shrimp, tails removed

DIRECTIONS

1. In a bowl, stir together water, ketchup, soy sauce, cornstarch, honey, crushed red pepper, and ground ginger. Set aside.
2. Heat oil in a large skillet over medium-high heat. Stir in green onions and garlic; cook 30 seconds. Stir in shrimp, and toss to coat with oil. Stir in sauce. Cook and stir until sauce is bubbly and thickened.

COLLEEN'S SLOW COOKER JAMBALAYA

Servings: 12 | Prep: 20m | Cooks: 8h | Total: 8h20m

NUTRITION FACTS

Calories: 234.6 | Carbohydrates: 6.1g | Protein: 20.2g | Cholesterol: 98.9mg | Sodium: 687.6mg

INGREDIENTS

- 1 pound Chicken, broilers or fryers, breast, meat only, raw
- 1 pound andouille sausage, pork and beef, cooked
- 1 (28 ounce) can S & W Ready Cut Tomatoes in Juice-Cnd-Cup SW
- 1 large Onions, raw
- 1 large Peppers, sweet, green, raw; green bell pepper
- 1 cup Celery, raw
- 1 cup Swanson Clear Chicken Broth CAM
- 2 teaspoons Spices, oregano, ground
- 2 teaspoons Spices, parsley, dried
- 2 teaspoons Cajun Seasoning LF
- 1 teaspoon Spices, pepper, red or cayenne
- 1/2 teaspoon Spices, thyme, dried
- 1 pound Shrimp, fresh, frozen, medium (31-35)

DIRECTIONS

1. In a slow cooker, mix the chicken, sausage, tomatoes with juice, onion, green bell pepper, celery, and broth. Season with oregano, parsley, Cajun seasoning, cayenne pepper, and thyme.
2. Cover, and cook 7 to 8 hours on Low, or 3 to 4 hours on High. Stir in the shrimp during the last 30 minutes of cook time.

SHRIMP SCAMPI BAKE

Servings: 6 | Prep: 30m | Cooks: 15m | Total: 45m

NUTRITION FACTS

Calories: 420.1 | Carbohydrates: 1.8g | Protein: 30g | Cholesterol: 320.5mg | Sodium: 681.2mg

INGREDIENTS

- 1 cup Butter, with salt
- 1 tablespoon Garlic, raw

- 2 tablespoons Dijon Mustard NB
- 1 tablespoon Lemon juice, raw

- 1 tablespoon Parsley, raw
- 2 pounds Crustaceans, shrimp, mixed species, raw

DIRECTIONS

1. Preheat oven to 450 degrees F (230 degrees C).
2. In a small saucepan over medium heat, combine the butter, mustard, lemon juice, garlic, and parsley. When the butter melts completely, remove from heat.
3. Arrange shrimp in a shallow baking dish. Pour the butter mixture over the shrimp.
4. Bake in preheated oven for 12 to 15 minutes or until the shrimp are pink and opaque.

PEPPERED SHRIMP ALFREDO

Servings: 6 | Prep: 30m | Cooks: 20m | Total: 50m

NUTRITION FACTS

Calories: 707 | Carbohydrates: 50.6g | Protein: 28.4g | Cholesterol: 201.5mg | Sodium: 1034.5mg

INGREDIENTS

- 12 ounces penne pasta, dry
- 1/4 cup Butter, with salt
- 2 tablespoons Extra Virgin Olive Oil NOI
- 1 Onions, raw
- 2 cloves Garlic, raw
- 1 Peppers, sweet, red, raw; red bell pepper
- 1/2pound Mushrooms, portobello, raw

- 1 pound Shrimp, fresh, raw, medium (31-35)
- 1 (15 ounce) jar Di Girono Alfredo Sauce KFT
- 1/2cup Cheese, pecorino romano
- 1/2 cup Cream, fluid, heavy whipping
- 1 teaspoon Spices, pepper, red or cayenne
- 1 pinch Salt, table
- 1/4 cup Parsley, raw

DIRECTIONS

1. Bring a large pot of lightly salted water to a boil. Add pasta and cook for 8 to 10 minutes or until al dente; drain.

2. Meanwhile, melt butter together with the olive oil in a saucepan over medium heat. Stir in onion, and cook until softened and translucent, about 2 minutes. Stir in garlic, red pepper, and mushroom; cook over medium-high heat until soft, about 2 minutes more.

3. Stir in the shrimp, and cook until firm and pink, then pour in Alfredo sauce, Romano cheese, and cream; bring to a simmer stirring constantly until thickened, about 5 minutes. Season with cayenne, salt, and pepper to taste. Stir drained pasta into the sauce, and serve sprinkled with chopped parsley.

COCONUT SHRIMP

Servings: 6 | Prep: 10m | Cooks: 20m | Total: 1h | Additional: 30m

NUTRITION FACTS

Calories: 316.6 | Carbohydrates: 26.3g | Protein: 8.4g | Cholesterol: 67.5mg | Sodium: 240.8mg

INGREDIENTS

- 1 Egg, whole, raw, fresh

- 1/2 cup Wheat flour, white, all-purpose, enriched, bleached

- 2/3 cup Alcoholic beverage, beer, regular

- 1 1/2 teaspoons Leavening agents, baking powder, double-acting, sodium aluminum sulfate

- 1/4 cup Wheat flour, white, all-purpose, enriched, bleached

- 2 cups Nuts, coconut meat, dried (desiccated), sweetened, flaked, packaged

- 24 Crustaceans, shrimp, mixed species, raw

- 3 cups oil for frying

DIRECTIONS

1. In medium bowl, combine egg, 1/2 cup flour, beer and baking powder. Place 1/4 cup flour and coconut in two separate bowls.

2. Hold shrimp by tail, and dredge in flour, shaking off excess flour. Dip in egg/beer batter; allow excess to drip off. Roll shrimp in coconut, and place on a baking sheet lined with wax paper. Refrigerate for 30 minutes. Meanwhile, heat oil to 350 degrees F (175 degrees C) in a deep-fryer.

3. Fry shrimp in batches: cook, turning once, for 2 to 3 minutes, or until golden brown. Using tongs, remove shrimp to paper towels to drain. Serve warm with your favorite dipping sauce.

SHRIMP LEMON PEPPER LINGUINI

Servings: 4 | Prep: 15m | Cooks: 25m | Total: 40m

NUTRITION FACTS

Calories: 483.7 | Carbohydrates: 47.7g | Protein: 31.6g | Cholesterol: 203.8mg | Sodium: 441.3mg

INGREDIENTS

- 1 (8 ounce) package GG Linguine Pasta Semolina-Dry-5/8"Crcl QK
- 1 tablespoon Oil, olive, salad or cooking
- 6 cloves Garlic, raw
- 1/2 cup Swanson Clear Chicken Broth CAM
- 1/4 cup Alcoholic beverage, wine, table, white
- 1 Lemons, raw, with peel
- 1/2 teaspoon Lemon peel, raw
- 1 pinch Salt, table
- 2 teaspoons Spices, pepper, black
- 1 pound Crustaceans, shrimp, mixed species, raw
- 1/4 cup Butter, with salt
- 3 tablespoons Parsley, raw
- 1 tablespoon Basil, fresh

DIRECTIONS

1. Bring a large pot of lightly salted water to a boil. Add linguine, and cook for 9 to 13 minutes or until al dente; drain.
2. Heat oil in a large saucepan over medium heat, and saute garlic about 1 minute. Mix in chicken broth, wine, lemon juice, lemon zest, salt, and pepper. Reduce heat, and simmer until liquid is reduced by about 1/2.
3. Mix shrimp, butter, parsley, and basil into the saucepan. Cook 2 to 3 minutes, until shrimp is opaque. Stir in the cooked linguine, and continue cooking 2 minutes, until well coated.

GRILLED MARINATED SHRIMP

Servings: 6 | Prep: 30m | Cooks: 10m | Total: 2h40m | Additional: 2h

NUTRITION FACTS

Calories: 447.1 | Carbohydrates: 3.7g | Protein: 25.3g | Cholesterol: 230.4mg | Sodium: 800mg

INGREDIENTS

- 1 cup Oil, olive, salad or cooking
- 1/4 cup Parsley, raw
- 1 Lemons, raw, with peel
- 2 tablespoons Sauce, ready-to-serve, pepper or hot
- 3 cloves Garlic, raw
- 1 tablespoon Tomato products, canned, paste, with salt added

- 2 teaspoons Spices, oregano, ground
- 1 teaspoon Salt, table
- 1 teaspoon Spices, pepper, black
- 2 pounds Crustaceans, shrimp, mixed species, raw
- 6 eaches Skewers

DIRECTIONS

1. In a mixing bowl, mix together olive oil, parsley, lemon juice, hot sauce, garlic, tomato paste, oregano, salt, and black pepper. Reserve a small amount for basting later. Pour remaining marinade into a large resealable plastic bag with shrimp. Seal, and marinate in the refrigerator for 2 hours.
2. Preheat grill for medium-low heat. Thread shrimp onto skewers, piercing once near the tail and once near the head. Discard marinade.
3. Lightly oil grill grate. Cook shrimp for 5 minutes per side, or until opaque, basting frequently with reserved marinade.

THE BEST THAI COCONUT SOUP

Servings: 8 | Prep: 35m | Cooks: 30m | Total: 1h5m

NUTRITION FACTS

Calories: 367.6 | Carbohydrates: 8.9g | Protein: 13.2g | Cholesterol: 86.3mg | Sodium: 579.4mg

INGREDIENTS

- 1 tablespoon Oil, soybean, salad or cooking
- 2 tablespoons Ginger root, raw
- 1 stalk Lemon grass (citronella), raw
- 2 teaspoons curry paste

- 3 (13.5 ounce) cans Nuts, coconut milk, canned (liquid expressed from grated meat and water)
- 1/2 pound Shiitake Mushrooms-Raw AMM
- 1 pound Shrimp, fresh, raw, medium (31-35)
- 2 tablespoons Lime juice, raw

- 4 cups Swanson Clear Chicken Broth CAM
- 3 tablespoons Sauce, fish, ready-to-serve
- 1 tablespoon Sugars, brown
- 1 pinch Salt, table
- 1/4 cup Cilantro, raw

DIRECTIONS

1. Heat the oil in a large pot over medium heat. Cook and stir the ginger, lemongrass, and curry paste in the heated oil for 1 minute. Slowly pour the chicken broth over the mixture, stirring continually. Stir in the fish sauce and brown sugar; simmer for 15 minutes. Stir in the coconut milk and mushrooms; cook and stir until the mushrooms are soft, about 5 minutes. Add the shrimp; cook until no longer translucent about 5 minutes. Stir in the lime juice; season with salt; garnish with cilantro.

SIMPLE GARLIC SHRIMP

Servings: 4 | Prep: 15m | Cooks: 10m | Total: 25m

NUTRITION FACTS

Calories: 196 | Carbohydrates: 2.9g | Fat: 12g | Protein: 19.1g | Cholesterol: 188mg | Sodium: 244mg

INGREDIENTS

- 1 1/2 tablespoons olive oil
- 1 pound shrimp, peeled and deveined
- salt to taste
- 6 cloves garlic, finely minced
- 1/4 teaspoon red pepper flakes
- 3 tablespoons lemon juice
- 1 tablespoon caper brine
- 1 1/2 teaspoons cold butter
- 1/3 cup chopped Italian flat leaf parsley, divided
- 1 1/2 tablespoons cold butter
- water, as needed

DIRECTIONS

1. Heat olive oil in a heavy skillet over high heat until it just begins to smoke. Place shrimp in an even layer on the bottom of the pan and cook for 1 minute without stirring.
2. Season shrimp with salt; cook and stir until shrimp begin to turn pink, about 1 minute.
3. Stir in garlic and red pepper flakes; cook and stir 1 minute. Stir in lemon juice, caper brine, 1 1/2 teaspoon cold butter, and half the parsley.

4. Cook until butter has melted, about 1 minute, then turn heat to low and stir in 1 1/2 tablespoon cold butter. Cook and stir until all butter has melted to form a thick sauce and shrimp are pink and opaque, about 2 to 3 minutes.
5. Remove shrimp with a slotted spoon and transfer to a bowl; continue to cook butter sauce, adding water 1 teaspoon at a time if too thick, about 2 minutes. Season with salt to taste.
6. Serve shrimp topped with the pan sauce. Garnish with remaining flat-leaf parsley.

CREAMY PESTO SHRIMP

Servings: 8 | Prep: 15m | Cooks: 15m | Total: 30m

NUTRITION FACTS

Calories: 646 | Carbohydrates: 43g | Protein: 23.1g | Cholesterol: 210.4mg | Sodium: 437.2mg

INGREDIENTS

- 1 pound GG Linguine Pasta Semolina-Dry-5/8"Crcl QK
- 1/2 cup Butter, with salt
- 2 cups Cream, fluid, heavy whipping
- 1/2 teaspoon Spices, pepper, black
- 1 cup Cheese, parmesan, grated
- 1/3 cup Pesto Sauce
- 1 pound Crustaceans, shrimp, mixed species, raw

DIRECTIONS

1. Bring a large pot of lightly salted water to a boil. Add linguine pasta, and cook for 8 to 10 minutes, or until al dente; drain.
2. In a large skillet, melt the butter over medium heat. Stir in cream, and season with pepper. Cook 6 to 8 minutes, stirring constantly.
3. Stir Parmesan cheese into cream sauce, stirring until thoroughly mixed. Blend in the pesto, and cook for 3 to 5 minutes, until thickened.
4. Stir in the shrimp, and cook until they turn pink, about 5 minutes. Serve over the hot linguine.

ANGEL HAIR PASTA WITH SHRIMP AND BASIL

Servings: 4 | Prep: 10m | Cooks: 25m | Total: 35m

NUTRITION FACTS

Calories: 526.6 | Carbohydrates: 46.7g | Protein: 34g | Cholesterol: 175.8mg | Sodium: 968.9mg

INGREDIENTS

- 1/4 cup Oil, olive, salad or cooking
- 1 (8 ounce) package Di Giorno Angel Hair Pasta-Dry KFT
- 1 teaspoon Garlic, raw
- 1 pound Crustaceans, shrimp, mixed species, raw
- 2 (28 ounce) cans Italn Styl Rdy Cut Tomatoes In Jce-Cnd-Cup SW
- 1/2 cup Alcoholic beverage, wine, table, white
- 1/4 cup Parsley, raw
- 3 tablespoons Basil, fresh
- 3 tablespoons Cheese, parmesan, grated

DIRECTIONS

1. Bring a large pot of water to a boil, and add 1 tablespoon oil. Cook pasta in boiling water until al dente. Place pasta in a colander, and give it a quick rinse with cold water.
2. Heat remaining olive oil in a 10 inch skillet over medium heat. Cook garlic, stirring constantly, until the garlic is tender, about 1 minute. Do not let the garlic burn. Add shrimp, and cook for 3 to 5 minutes. Remove shrimp from the skillet, and set aside.
3. Stir tomatoes, wine, parsley, and basil into the skillet. Continue cooking, stirring occasionally, until liquid is reduced by half, 8 to 12 minutes. Add shrimp, and continue cooking until the shrimp are heated through, about 2 to 3 minutes. Serve the shrimp mixture over the pasta. Sprinkle with Parmesan cheese.

SHRIMP SCAMPI

Servings: 4 | Prep: 15m | Cooks: 10m | Total: 25m

NUTRITION FACTS

Calories: 605.6 | Carbohydrates: 35.5g | Protein: 35.3g | Cholesterol: 246.7mg | Sodium: 680.1mg

INGREDIENTS

- 1 (8 ounce) package Di Giorno Angel Hair Pasta-Dry KFT
- 1/2 cup Butter, with salt
- 4 cloves Garlic, raw
- 1 cup Burgundy Wine
- 1/4 teaspoon Spices, pepper, black
- 3/4 cup Cheese, parmesan, grated

- 1 pound Crustaceans, shrimp, mixed species, raw
- 1 tablespoon Parsley, raw

DIRECTIONS

1. Bring a large pot of salted water to a boil. Stir in pasta and return pot to boil. Cook until al dente. Drain well.
2. Melt butter in a large saucepan over medium heat. Stir in garlic and shrimp. Cook, stirring constantly, for 3 to 5 minutes.
3. Stir in wine and pepper. Bring to a boil and cook for 30 seconds while stirring constantly.
4. Mix shrimp with drained pasta in a serving bowl. Sprinkle with cheese and parsley. Serve immediately.

SHRIMP SCAMPI WITH PASTA

Servings: 6 | Prep: 20m | Cooks: 20m | Total: 40m

NUTRITION FACTS

Calories: 511.4 | Carbohydrates: 57.5g | Protein: 21.9g | Cholesterol: 135.4mg | Sodium: 260mg

INGREDIENTS

- 1 (16 ounce) package GG Linguine Pasta Semolina-Dry-5/8"Crcl QK
- 2 tablespoons Butter, with salt
- 2 tablespoons Extra Virgin Olive Oil NOI
- 2 eaches Shallots, raw
- 2 cloves Garlic, raw
- 1 pinch dried red pepper flakes
- 1 pound Crustaceans, shrimp, mixed species, raw
- 1 pinch Morton Kosher Salt, coarse
- 1/2 cup Alcoholic beverage, wine, table, white
- 1 Lemon juice, raw
- 2 tablespoons Butter, with salt
- 2 tablespoons Extra Virgin Olive Oil NOI
- 1/4 cup Parsley, raw
- 1 teaspoon Extra Virgin Olive Oil NOI

DIRECTIONS

1. Bring a large pot of salted water to a boil; cook linguine in boiling water until nearly tender, 6 to 8 minutes. Drain.

2. Melt 2 tablespoons butter with 2 tablespoons olive oil in a large skillet over medium heat. Cook and stir shallots, garlic, and red pepper flakes in the hot butter and oil until shallots are translucent, 3 to 4 minutes. Season shrimp with kosher salt and black pepper; add to the skillet and cook until pink, stirring occasionally, 2 to 3 minutes. Remove shrimp from skillet and keep warm.

3. Pour white wine and lemon juice into skillet and bring to a boil while scraping the browned bits of food off of the bottom of the skillet with a wooden spoon. Melt 2 tablespoons butter in skillet, stir 2 tablespoons olive oil into butter mixture, and bring to a simmer. Toss linguine, shrimp, and parsley in the butter mixture until coated; season with salt and black pepper. Drizzle with 1 teaspoon olive oil to serve.

SHRIMP AND MUSHROOM LINGUINI WITH CREAMY CHEESE HERB SAUCE

Servings: 4 | Prep: 15m | Cooks: 15m | Total: 30m

NUTRITION FACTS

Calories: 601.4 | Carbohydrates: 44g | Protein: 23.2g | Cholesterol: 210.3mg | Sodium: 402.7mg

INGREDIENTS

- 1 (8 ounce) package GG Linguine Pasta Semolina-Dry-5/8"Crcl QK
- 2 tablespoons Butter, with salt
- 1/2pound Mushrooms, raw
- 1/2cup Butter, with salt
- 2 cloves Garlic, raw

- 1 (3 ounce) package Cheese, cream
- 2 tablespoons Parsley, raw
- 3/4 teaspoon Spices, basil, ground
- 2/3 cup Water, municipal
- 1/2 pound Crustaceans, shrimp, mixed species, cooked, moist heat

DIRECTIONS

1. Bring a large pot of lightly salted water to a boil. Add linguini and cook until tender, about 7 minutes. Drain.

2. Meanwhile, heat 2 tablespoons butter in a large skillet over medium-high heat. Add mushrooms; cook and stir until tender. Transfer to a plate.

3. In the same pan, melt 1/2 cup butter with the minced garlic. Stir in the cream cheese, breaking it up with a spoon as it melts. Stir in the parsley and basil. Simmer for 5 minutes. Mix in boiling water until sauce is smooth. Stir in cooked shrimp and mushrooms; heat sauce through.

4. Toss linguini with shrimp sauce and serve.

SPICY GRILLED SHRIMP

Servings: 6 | Prep: 15m | Cooks: 6m | Total: 21m

NUTRITION FACTS

Calories: 164 | Carbohydrates: 2.7g | Protein: 25.1g | Cholesterol: 230mg | Sodium: 586mg

INGREDIENTS

- 1 large clove garlic
- 1 teaspoon coarse salt
- 1/2 teaspoon cayenne pepper
- 1 teaspoon paprika
- 2 tablespoons olive oil
- 2 teaspoons lemon juice
- 2 pounds large shrimp, peeled and deveined
- 8 wedges lemon, for garnish

DIRECTIONS

1. Preheat grill for medium heat.
2. In a small bowl, crush the garlic with the salt. Mix in cayenne pepper and paprika, and then stir in olive oil and lemon juice to form a paste. In a large bowl, toss shrimp with garlic paste until evenly coated.
3. Lightly oil grill grate. Cook shrimp for 2 to 3 minutes per side, or until opaque. Transfer to a serving dish, garnish with lemon wedges, and serve.

GOOD NEW ORLEANS CREOLE GUMBO

Servings: 20 | Prep: 1h | Cooks: 2h40m | Total: 3h40m

NUTRITION FACTS

Calories: 283.1 | Carbohydrates: 12.1g | Protein: 20.9g | Cholesterol: 142.6mg | Sodium: 853.1mg

INGREDIENTS

- 1 cup Wheat flour, white, all-purpose, enriched, bleached
- 3/4 cup Bacon Grease/Meat Drippings
- 1 cup Celery, raw
- 1 large Onions, raw
- 4 eaches Spices, bay leaf, crumbled
- 1/2 teaspoon Spices, thyme, dried
- 1 (14.5 ounce) can Tomatoes, red, ripe, canned, stewed
- 1 (6 ounce) can Contadina Tomato Sauce-

- 1 large Peppers, sweet, green, raw; green bell pepper
- 2 cloves Garlic, raw
- 1 pound andouille sausage, pork and beef, cooked
- 3 quarts Water, municipal
- 6 cubes Soup, beef broth, cubed, dry
- 1 tablespoon Sugars, granulated
- 1 pinch Salt, table
- 2 tablespoons Sauce, ready-to-serve, pepper or hot
- 1/2teaspoon Cajun Seasoning LF

- 2 teaspoons file powder (powdered sassafras leaves)
- 2 tablespoons Bacon Grease/Meat Drippings
- 2 (10 ounce) packages Okra, raw
- 2 tablespoons Distilled Vinegar
- 1 pound Crustaceans, crab, dungeness, cooked, moist heat
- 3 pounds Shrimp, fresh, raw, medium (31-35)
- 2 tablespoons Worcestershire Sauce
- 2 teaspoons file powder (powdered sassafras leaves)

DIRECTIONS

1. Make a roux by whisking the flour and 3/4 cup bacon drippings together in a large, heavy saucepan over medium-low heat to form a smooth mixture. Cook the roux, whisking constantly, until it turns a rich mahogany brown color. This can take 20 to 30 minutes; watch heat carefully and whisk constantly or roux will burn. Remove from heat; continue whisking until mixture stops cooking.
2. Place the celery, onion, green bell pepper, and garlic into the work bowl of a food processor, and pulse until the vegetables are very finely chopped. Stir the vegetables into the roux, and mix in the sausage. Bring the mixture to a simmer over medium-low heat, and cook until vegetables are tender, 10 to 15 minutes. Remove from heat, and set aside.
3. Bring the water and beef bouillon cubes to a boil in a large Dutch oven or soup pot. Stir until the bouillon cubes dissolve, and whisk the roux mixture into the boiling water. Reduce heat to a simmer, and mix in the sugar, salt, hot pepper sauce, Cajun seasoning, bay leaves, thyme, stewed tomatoes, and tomato sauce. Simmer the soup over low heat for 1 hour; mix in 2 teaspoons of file gumbo powder at the 45-minute mark.
4. Meanwhile, melt 2 tablespoons of bacon drippings in a skillet, and cook the okra with vinegar over medium heat for 15 minutes; remove okra with slotted spoon, and stir into the simmering gumbo. Mix in crabmeat, shrimp, and Worcestershire sauce, and simmer until flavors have blended, 45 more minutes. Just before serving, stir in 2 more teaspoons of file gumbo powder.

BASIL SHRIMP

Servings: 9 | Prep: 25m | Cooks: 5m | Total: 1h30m | Additional: 1h

NUTRITION FACTS

Calories: 205.7 | Carbohydrates: 2.4g | Protein: 25g | Cholesterol: 243.9mg | Sodium: 426.9mg

INGREDIENTS

- 2 1/2tablespoons Oil, olive, salad or cooking
- 1/4 cup Butter, with salt
- 1 1/2 Lemons, raw, without peel
- 3 tablespoons Dijon Mustard NB
- 1/2cup Basil, fresh
- 3 cloves Garlic, raw
- 1 pinch Salt, table
- 1 pinch Spices, pepper, white
- 3 pounds Crustaceans, shrimp, mixed species, raw
- 4 eaches Skewers

DIRECTIONS

1. In a shallow, non-porous dish or bowl, mix together olive oil and melted butter. Stir in lemon juice, mustard, basil, and garlic, and season with salt and white pepper. Add shrimp, and toss to coat. Cover, and refrigerate for 1 hour.
2. Preheat grill to high heat. Remove shrimp from marinade, and thread onto skewers. Discard marinade.
3. Lightly oil grill grate, and arrange skewers on preheated grill. Cook for 4 minutes, turning once, or until opaque.

OLD CHARLESTON STYLE SHRIMP AND GRITS

Servings: 4 | Prep: 30m | Cooks: 45m | Total: 1h15m

NUTRITION FACTS

Calories: 618 | Carbohydrates: 16.2g | Fat: 43.7g | Protein: 38.6g | Cholesterol: 270mg

INGREDIENTS

- 1 cup coarsely ground grits
- 3 cups water
- 2 teaspoons salt
- 1 green bell pepper, chopped
- 1 red bell pepper, chopped
- 1 yellow bell pepper, chopped

- 2 cups half-and-half
- 2 pounds uncooked shrimp, peeled and deveined
- salt to taste
- 1 pinch cayenne pepper, or to taste
- 1 lemon, juiced
- 1 pound andouille sausage, cut into 1/4-inch slices
- 5 slices bacon
- 1 cup chopped onion
- 1 teaspoon minced garlic
- 1/4 cup butter
- 1/4 cup all-purpose flour
- 1 cup chicken broth
- 1 tablespoon Worcestershire sauce
- 1 cup shredded sharp Cheddar cheese

DIRECTIONS

1. Bring water, grits, and salt to a boil in a heavy saucepan with a lid. Stir in half-and-half and simmer until grits are thickened and tender, 15 to 20 minutes. Set aside and keep warm.
2. Sprinkle shrimp with salt and cayenne pepper; drizzle with lemon juice. Set aside in a bowl.
3. Place andouille sausage slices in a large skillet over medium heat; fry sausage until browned, 5 to 8 minutes. Remove skillet from heat.
4. Cook bacon in a large skillet over medium-high heat, turning occasionally, until evenly browned, about 10 minutes. Retain bacon drippings in skillet. Transfer bacon slices to paper towels, let cool, and crumble.
5. Cook and stir green, red, and yellow bell peppers, onion, and garlic in the bacon drippings until the onion is translucent, about 8 minutes.
6. Stir shrimp and cooked vegetables into the andouille sausage and mix to combine.
7. Melt butter in a saucepan over medium heat; stir in flour to make a smooth paste. Turn heat to low and cook, stirring constantly, until the mixture is medium brown in color, 8 to 10 minutes. Watch carefully, mixture burns easily.
8. Pour the butter-flour mixture into the skillet with andouille sausage, shrimp, and vegetables. Place the skillet over medium heat and pour in chicken broth, bacon and Worcestershire sauce, cooking and stirring until the sauce thickens and the shrimp become opaque and bright pink, about 8 minutes.
9. Just before serving, mix sharp Cheddar cheese into grits until melted and grits are creamy and light yellow. Serve shrimp mixture over cheese grits.

BUBBA'S JAMBALAYA

Servings: 12 | Prep: 25m | Cooks: 40m | Total: 1h5m

NUTRITION FACTS

Calories: 348.5 | Carbohydrates: 32.3g | Protein: 22.7g | Cholesterol: 72.4mg | Sodium: 1176.5mg

INGREDIENTS

- 6 slices Pork, cured, bacon, raw
- 1 cup Celery, raw
- 1 Peppers, sweet, green, raw; green bell pepper
- 1 Onions, raw
- 1/2 pound cooked ham meat
- 1/2pound Chicken, broilers or fryers, breast, meat and skin, cooked, stewed
- 1/2pound Smoked link sausage, pork
- 2 (14.5 ounce) cans Tomatoes, crushed, canned
- 2 cups Soup, beef broth or bouillon canned, ready-to-serve
- 2 cups Swanson Clear Chicken Broth CAM
- 1 teaspoon Spices, thyme, dried
- 2 teaspoons Cajun Seasoning LF
- 2 cups Rice, white, long-grain, regular, raw, enriched
- 1/2pound Shrimp, fresh, frozen, small (36-45)

DIRECTIONS

1. Heat a large pot over medium-high heat. Add bacon, and cook until crisp. Remove bacon pieces with a slotted spoon, and set aside. Add celery, bell pepper, and onion to the bacon drippings, and cook until tender.
2. Add the ham, chicken and sausage to the pot, and pour in the tomatoes, beef broth and chicken broth. Season with thyme and Cajun seasoning. Bring to a boil, and add the rice. Bring to a boil, then turn the heat to low, cover, and simmer for about 20 minutes, until the rice is tender.
3. Stir in the shrimp and bacon just before serving, and heat through. If you use uncooked shrimp, let it cook for about 5 minutes before serving.

GARLIC SHRIMP LINGUINE

Servings: 8 | Prep: 10m | Cooks: 20m | Total: 30m

NUTRITION FACTS

Calories: 287 | Carbohydrates: 42.3g | Fat: 4.9g | Protein: 17.6g | Cholesterol: 77mg | Sodium: 126mg

INGREDIENTS

- 1 pound uncooked linguine
- 1 tablespoon butter
- 3 cloves garlic, minced
- 1 teaspoon chopped fresh parsley

- 3 tablespoons white wine
- 2 teaspoons grated Parmesan cheese
- 1 pinch salt and pepper to taste
- 1 pound medium shrimp, peeled and deveined

DIRECTIONS

1. Bring a large pot of lightly salted water to a boil. Add pasta and cook for 8 to 10 minutes or until al dente; drain.
2. In a medium saucepan, melt butter over medium low heat; add wine, cheese, garlic, parsley and salt and pepper to taste. Simmer over low heat for 3 to 5 minutes, stirring frequently.
3. Increase heat to medium high and add shrimp to saucepan; cook for about 3 to 4 minutes or until shrimp begins to turn pink. Do not overcook.
4. Divide pasta into portions and spoon sauce on top; garnish with Parmesan cheese and fresh parsley, if desired.

HAPPY SHRIMP

Servings: 4 | Prep: 20m | Cooks: 20m | Total: 40m

NUTRITION FACTS

Calories: 280 | Carbohydrates: 3.1g | Fat: 19.9g | Protein: 19.5g | Cholesterol: 230mg | Sodium: 330mg

INGREDIENTS

- 1/4 cup butter
- 1 1/2 teaspoons minced garlic
- 1 pound peeled and deveined medium shrimp
- 1/4 cup chopped green onions
- 1/4 cup dry white wine
- 1/3 cup heavy cream
- 2 tablespoons chopped fresh basil
- 2 roma (plum) tomatoes, chopped
- 1 pinch cayenne pepper, or to taste
- salt and pepper to taste

DIRECTIONS

1. Melt the butter in a large skillet over medium-high heat. Stir in the shrimp, garlic, and green onions. Cook and stir until the shrimp are pink on the outside, and no longer translucent in the center, about 5 minutes. Set the shrimp aside, and pour in the wine, cream, tomatoes, basil, and cayenne pepper. Bring to a simmer, then reduce heat to medium-low, and simmer until the sauce will coat the back of a spoon, about 10 minutes.
2. Stir the shrimp back into the sauce, and season to taste with salt and pepper. Heat through and serve.

SHRIMP FETTUCCINE ALFREDO

Servings: 6 | Prep: 20m | Cooks: 20m | Total: 40m

NUTRITION FACTS

Calories: 440.2 | Carbohydrates: 57.7g | Protein: 29.2g | Cholesterol: 172mg | Sodium: 280.7mg

INGREDIENTS

- 1 pound GG Fettucine Pasta Semol-Dry-3/8"Crcl QK
- 1 tablespoon Butter, with salt
- 1 pound Crustaceans, shrimp, mixed species, cooked, moist heat
- 4 cloves Garlic, raw
- 1 cup Cream, fluid, half and half
- 6 tablespoons Cheese, parmesan, grated
- 1 tablespoon Parsley, raw
- Salt, table

DIRECTIONS

1. Bring a large pot of lightly salted water to a boil. Add pasta and cook for 8 to 10 minutes or until al dente; drain.
2. In a large skillet, cook and stir shrimp and garlic in the butter for about one minute. Pour in half and half; stir. Sprinkle Parmesan cheese in one tablespoon at a time, stirring constantly. After all Parmesan is added, mix in parsley and salt. Stir frequently making sure it does not boil. Sauce will take a while to thicken.
3. When sauce has thickened, combine with cooked pasta noodles; serve hot.

GRILLED SHRIMP SCAMPI

Servings: 6 | Prep: 30m | Cooks: 6m | Total: 36m

NUTRITION FACTS

Calories: 173.1 | Carbohydrates: 1.6g | Protein: 18.7g | Cholesterol: 172.6mg | Sodium: 199.9mg

INGREDIENTS

- 1/4cup Oil, olive, salad or cooking
- 1/4 cup Lemon juice, raw
- 3 tablespoons Parsley, raw
- 1/4teaspoon Spices, pepper, black
- 1/4teaspoon dried red pepper flakes
- 1 1/2 pounds Crustaceans, shrimp, mixed species,

raw

- 1 tablespoon Garlic, raw

DIRECTIONS

1. In a large, non-reactive bowl, stir together the olive oil, lemon juice, parsley, garlic, and black pepper. Season with crushed red pepper, if desired. Add shrimp, and toss to coat. Marinate in the refrigerator for 30 minutes.
2. Preheat grill for high heat. Thread shrimp onto skewers, piercing once near the tail and once near the head. Discard any remaining marinade.
3. Lightly oil grill grate. Grill for 2 to 3 minutes per side, or until opaque.

CIOPPINO

Servings: 13 | Prep: 10m | Cooks: 45m | Total: 55m

NUTRITION FACTS

Calories: 317.5 | Carbohydrates: 9.3g | Protein: 34.9g | Cholesterol: 163.9mg | Sodium: 755mg

INGREDIENTS

- 3/4 cup Butter, with salt
- 2 Onions, raw
- 2 cloves Garlic, raw
- 1 bunch Parsley, raw
- 2 (14.5 ounce) cans Tomatoes, red, ripe, canned, stewed
- 2 (14.5 ounce) cans Swanson Clear Chicken Broth CAM
- 2 Spices, bay leaf, crumbled
- 1 tablespoon Spices, basil, ground
- 1/2teaspoon Spices, thyme, dried

- 1/2 teaspoon Spices, oregano, ground
- 1 cup Water, municipal
- 1 1/2cups Alcoholic beverage, wine, table, white
- 1 1/2pounds Crustaceans, shrimp, mixed species, raw
- 1 1/2pounds sea scallops, raw
- 18 small Clam, mixed species, raw
- 18 Mollusks, mussel, blue, raw
- 1 1/2cups Crab, canned
- 1 1/2pounds Finfish, cod, Atlantic, raw

DIRECTIONS

1. Over medium-low heat melt butter in a large stockpot, add onions, garlic and parsley. Cook slowly, stirring occasionally until onions are soft.
2. Add tomatoes to the pot (break them into chunks as you add them). Add chicken broth, bay leaves, basil, thyme, oregano, water and wine. Mix well. Cover and simmer 30 minutes.
3. Stir in the shrimp, scallops, clams, mussels and crabmeat. Stir in fish, if desired. Bring to boil. Lower heat, cover and simmer 5 to 7 minutes until clams open. Ladle soup into bowls and serve with warm, crusty bread!

CINDY'S JAMBALAYA

Servings: 8 | Prep: 20m | Cooks: 45m | Total: 1h10m | Additional: 5m

NUTRITION FACTS

Calories: 283.7 | Carbohydrates: 24.6g | Protein: 18.4g | Cholesterol: 106.8mg | Sodium: 889.2mg

INGREDIENTS

- 1 tablespoon Oil, olive, salad or cooking
- 1/2 pound Smoked link sausage, pork
- 1 large Onions, raw
- 1 cup Peppers, sweet, green, raw; green bell pepper
- 1 cup Celery, raw
- 1 pinch Salt, table
- 1/2 teaspoon Cajun Seasoning LF
- 1 cup Rice, white, long-grain, regular, raw, enriched
- 1 (14.5 ounce) can S & W Ready Cut Tomatoes in Juice-Cnd-Cup SW
- 1 tablespoon Garlic, raw
- 2 cups Swanson Clear Chicken Broth CAM
- 3 Spices, bay leaf, crumbled
- 1/4 teaspoon Spices, thyme, dried
- 1 pound Shrimp, fresh, raw, medium (31-35)

DIRECTIONS

1. Heat the olive oil in a Dutch oven or large pot over medium heat. Stir in the sausage, and cook for 2 minutes. Add the onion, bell pepper, and celery; season with salt and Cajun seasoning. Cook and stir until the vegetables are soft, 6 to 8 minutes. Stir in the rice until evenly coated in the vegetable mixture, then pour in the tomatoes with juice, garlic, chicken broth, bay leaves, and thyme leaves. Bring to a simmer over medium-high heat, then reduce heat to medium-low, cover, and simmer 20 minutes.

2. After 20 minutes, stir in the shrimp, and cook 10 minutes uncovered until the shrimp turn pink and are no longer translucent in the center. Remove the pot from the heat, and let stand 5 minutes. Discard the bay leaves before serving.

BAKED COCONUT SHRIMP

Servings: 4 | Prep: 15m | Cooks: 15m | Total: 30m

NUTRITION FACTS

Calories: 310 | Carbohydrates: 29.3g | Fat: 11.4g | Protein: g | Cholesterol: 173mg | Sodium: 928mg

INGREDIENTS

- 1 pound large shrimp, peeled and deveined
- 1/3 cup cornstarch
- 1 teaspoon salt
- 3/4 teaspoon cayenne pepper
- 2 cups flaked sweetened coconut
- 3 egg whites, beaten until foamy

DIRECTIONS

1. Preheat an oven to 400 degrees F (200 degrees C). Lightly coat a baking sheet with cooking spray.
2. Rinse and dry shrimp with paper towels. Mix cornstarch, salt, and cayenne pepper in a shallow bow; pour coconut flakes in a separate shallow bowl. Working with one shrimp at a time, dredge it in the cornstarch mixture, then dip it in the egg white, and roll it in the coconut, making sure to coat the shrimp well. Place on the prepared baking sheet, and repeat with the remaining shrimp.
3. Bake the shrimp until they are bright pink on the outside and the meat is no longer transparent in the center and the coconut is browned, 15 to 20 minutes, flipping the shrimp halfway through.

FRA DIAVOLO SAUCE WITH PASTA

Servings: 8 | Prep: 20m | Cooks: 40m | Total: 1h

NUTRITION FACTS

Calories: 334.7 | Carbohydrates: 46.3g | Protein: 18.7g | Cholesterol: 51.8mg | Sodium: 655mg

INGREDIENTS

- 4 tablespoons Oil, olive, salad or cooking
- 6 cloves Garlic, raw
- 1 (16 ounce) package GG Linguine Pasta Semolina-Dry-5/8"Crcl QK
- 8 ounces Crustaceans, shrimp, mixed species, raw

- 3 cups Tomatoes, red, ripe, canned, whole, regular pack
- 1 1/2 teaspoons Salt, table
- 1 teaspoon dried red pepper flakes
- 8 ounces sea scallops, raw
- 1 tablespoon Parsley, raw

DIRECTIONS

1. In a large saucepan, heat 2 tablespoons of the olive oil with the garlic over medium heat. When the garlic starts to sizzle, pour in the tomatoes. Season with salt and red pepper. Bring to a boil. Lower the heat, and simmer for 30 minutes, stirring occasionally.
2. Meanwhile, bring a large pot of lightly salted water to a boil. Cook pasta for 8 to 10 minutes, or until al dente; drain.
3. In a large skillet, heat the remaining 2 tablespoons of olive oil over high heat. Add the shrimp and scallops. Cook for about 2 minutes, stirring frequently, or until the shrimp turn pink. Add shrimp and scallops to the tomato mixture, and stir in the parsley. Cook for 3 to 4 minutes, or until the sauce just begins to bubble. Serve sauce over pasta.

SAUSAGE & SHRIMP JAMBALAYA

Servings: 4 | Prep: 15m | Cooks: 1h | Total: 1h15m

NUTRITION FACTS

Calories: 495 | Carbohydrates: 37.3g | Fat: 25.2g | Protein: 30.3g | Cholesterol: 221mg

INGREDIENTS

- 2 tablespoons butter
- 8 ounces andouille sausage, cut into 1/4-inch slices
- 2 tablespoons ground paprika
- 1 tablespoon ground cumin
- 1/2 teaspoon cayenne pepper
- 1/2 cup diced tomatoes
- 1 large green bell pepper, diced
- 4 green onions, thinly sliced
- 1 teaspoon salt
- 1 bay leaf
- 1 cup uncooked brown rice
- 3 cups chicken stock
- 1 pound large shrimp, peeled and deveined
- salt and ground black pepper to taste

- 2 stalks celery, sliced 1/4 inch thick

DIRECTIONS

1. Place butter and sausage in a large stockpot over medium heat; cook and stir for 5-6 minutes until sausage begins to brown.
2. Stir in paprika, cumin and cayenne; cook for 1 minute.
3. Stir tomatoes, celery, green pepper, green onions, salt, and bay leaf into sausage mixture.
4. Add brown rice and stir to combine. Stir in chicken stock and turn heat to low. Cover and cook for until rice is just tender, about 45 minutes.
5. Stir in shrimp, replace lid and cook for 5 minutes. Season with salt and black pepper.

CHAMPAGNE SHRIMP AND PASTA

Servings: 4 | Prep: 15m | Cooks: 15m | Total: 30m

NUTRITION FACTS

Calories: 607.5 | Carbohydrates: 38.9g | Protein: 31.5g | Cholesterol: 254mg | Sodium: 459.1mg

INGREDIENTS

- 8 ounces Di Giorno Angel Hair Pasta-Dry KFT
- 1 tablespoon Extra Virgin Olive Oil NOI
- 1 cup Mushrooms, raw
- 1 pound Crustaceans, shrimp, mixed species, raw
- 1 1/2 cups champagne
- 1/4 teaspoon Salt, table
- 2 tablespoons Shallots, raw
- 2 roma (plum) tomato
- 1 cup Cream, fluid, heavy whipping
- Salt, table
- 3 tablespoons Parsley, raw
- Cheese, parmesan, grated

DIRECTIONS

1. Bring a large pot of lightly salted water to a boil. Cook pasta in boiling water for 6 to 8 minutes or until al dente; drain.
2. Meanwhile, heat oil over medium-high heat in a large frying pan. Cook and stir mushrooms in oil until tender. Remove mushrooms from pan, and set aside.
3. Combine shrimp, champagne, and salt in the frying pan, and cook over high heat. When liquid just begins to boil, remove shrimp from pan. Add shallots and tomatoes to champagne; boil until liquid is

reduced to 1/2 cup, about 8 minutes. Stir in 3/4 cup cream; boil until slightly thick, about 1 to 2 minutes. Add shrimp and mushrooms to sauce, and heat through. Adjust seasonings to taste.

4. Toss hot, cooked pasta with remaining 1/4 cup cream and parsley. To serve, spoon shrimp with sauce over pasta, and top with Parmesan cheese.

SHRIMP AND ASPARAGUS

Servings: 8 | Prep: 20m | Cooks: 30m | Total: 50m

NUTRITION FACTS

Calories: | Carbohydrates: g | Fat: g | Protein: g | Cholesterol: mg

INGREDIENTS

- 1 pound Asparagus, raw
- 1 (16 ounce) package Noodles, egg, dry, enriched
- 4 cloves Garlic, raw
- 1/2 cup Extra Virgin Olive Oil NOI
- 1 cup Butter, with salt
- 1 tablespoon Lemon juice, raw
- 1 pound Crustaceans, shrimp, mixed species, raw
- 1 pound Mushrooms, raw
- 1/2 cup Cheese, parmesan, grated
- Salt, table

DIRECTIONS

1. In a small saucepan, boil or steam asparagus in enough water to cover until tender; chop and set aside.
2. Bring a large pot of salted water to full boil, place the pasta in the pot and return to a rolling boil; cook until al dente. Drain well.
3. In a large saucepan, saute garlic in the olive oil over medium-low heat until the garlic is golden brown.
4. Place butter and lemon juice in the saucepan. Heat until the butter has melted. Place the shrimp in the saucepan and cook until the shrimp turns pink. Place the mushrooms and asparagus into the saucepan, cook until mushrooms are tender.
5. Toss the shrimp and vegetable mixture with the egg noodles and sprinkle with Parmesan cheese. Salt and pepper to taste. Serve immediately.

EASY PAELLA

Servings: 8 | Prep: 30m | Cooks: 30m | Total: 1h

NUTRITION FACTS

Calories: 736.2 | Carbohydrates: 45.7g | Protein: 55.7g | Cholesterol: 202.5mg | Sodium: 1204.2mg

INGREDIENTS

- 2 tablespoons Oil, olive, salad or cooking
- 1 tablespoon Spices, paprika
- 2 teaspoons Spices, oregano, ground
- 1 pinch Salt, table
- 2 pounds Chicken, broilers or fryers, breast, meat only, raw
- 2 tablespoons Oil, olive, salad or cooking
- 3 cloves Garlic, raw
- 1 teaspoon dried red pepper flakes
- 2 cups Rice, white, short-grain, raw
- 1 pinch Spices, saffron
- 1 Spices, bay leaf, crumbled
- 1/2 bunch Italian flat leaf parsley
- 1 quart Chicken Stock-Dry-Prepared EFC
- 2 Lemon peel, raw
- 2 tablespoons Oil, olive, salad or cooking
- 1 Onions, raw
- 1 Peppers, sweet, red, raw; red bell pepper
- 1 pound Chorizo, pork and beef
- 1 pound Shrimp, fresh, raw, medium (31-35)

DIRECTIONS

1. In a medium bowl, mix together 2 tablespoons olive oil, paprika, oregano, and salt and pepper. Stir in chicken pieces to coat. Cover, and refrigerate.
2. Heat 2 tablespoons olive oil in a large skillet or paella pan over medium heat. Stir in garlic, red pepper flakes, and rice. Cook, stirring, to coat rice with oil, about 3 minutes. Stir in saffron threads, bay leaf, parsley, chicken stock, and lemon zest. Bring to a boil, cover, and reduce heat to medium low. Simmer 20 minutes.
3. Meanwhile, heat 2 tablespoons olive oil in a separate skillet over medium heat. Stir in marinated chicken and onion; cook 5 minutes. Stir in bell pepper and sausage; cook 5 minutes. Stir in shrimp; cook, turning the shrimp, until both sides are pink.
4. Spread rice mixture onto a serving tray. Top with meat and seafood mixture.

SHRIMP FRANCESCA

Servings: 4 | Prep: 20m | Cooks: 15m | Total: 35m

NUTRITION FACTS

Calories: 391.1 | Carbohydrates: 18.2g | Protein: 23.6g | Cholesterol: 235.5mg | Sodium: 940.2mg

INGREDIENTS

- 1 pound Shrimp, fresh, raw, large (21-30)
- 1 (8 ounce) can Artichoke Hearts In Water-Cnd CMF
- 1/2cup Progresso Italian Style Bread Crumbs PLB
- 1 tablespoon Parsley, raw
- 1 Lemon juice, raw
- 1/2 cup Butter, with salt
- 1 1/2tablespoons Garlic, raw
- 1 tablespoon Cheese, pecorino romano

DIRECTIONS

1. Preheat oven to 375 degrees F (190 degrees C). Lightly grease a 9x13-inch baking dish.
2. Arrange the shrimp in the bottom of the prepared baking dish. Gently squeeze any excess liquid from the artichoke hearts, break the hearts into quarters, and arrange in spaces between the shrimp. Sprinkle the bread crumbs and parsley over the shrimp and artichoke hearts; sprinkle lemon juice over the crumbs.
3. Melt butter with garlic in a small saucepan over medium-low heat; drizzle the butter mixture over the bread crumbs. Sprinkle the top with Romano cheese.
4. Bake in the preheated oven until the crumbs and cheese brown lightly and the shrimp turn opaque and orange-pink in color, 10 to 12 minutes. Serve hot.

CAJUN CRAWFISH AND SHRIMP ETOUFFE

Servings: 6 | Prep: 20m | Cooks: 50m | Total: 1h10m

NUTRITION FACTS

Calories: 264.2 | Carbohydrates: 9g | Protein: 24.9g | Cholesterol: 195.9mg | Sodium: 955.5mg

INGREDIENTS

- 1/3 cup Oil, soybean, salad or cooking
- 1/4 cup Wheat flour, white, all-purpose,
- 2 tablespoons Sauce, ready-to-serve, pepper or hot
- 1/3 teaspoon Spices, pepper, red or cayenne

enriched, bleached

- 1 small Peppers, sweet, green, raw; green bell pepper
- 1 medium Onions, raw
- 2 cloves Garlic, raw
- 2 stalks Celery, raw
- 2 Tomatoes, red, ripe, raw

- 2 tablespoons seafood seasoning
- 1/2 teaspoon Spices, pepper, black
- 1 cup Fish Broth/Stock
- 1 pound Crustaceans, crayfish, mixed species, farmed, raw
- 1 pound Shrimp, fresh, raw, medium (31-35)

DIRECTIONS

1. Heat the oil in a heavy skillet over medium heat. Gradually stir in flour, and stir constantly until the mixture turns 'peanut butter' brown or darker, at least 15 or 20 minutes. I use a large fork with the flat side to the bottom of the pan in a side to side motion. This is your base sauce or 'Roux'. It is very important to stir this constantly. If by chance the roux burns, discard and start over.
2. Once the roux is browned, add the onions, garlic, celery and bell pepper to the skillet, and saute for about 5 minutes to soften. Stir in the chopped tomatoes and fish stock, and season with the seafood seasoning. Reduce heat to low, and simmer for about 20 minutes, stirring occasionally.
3. Season the sauce with hot pepper sauce and cayenne pepper (if using), and add the crawfish and shrimp. Cook for about 10 minutes, or until the shrimp are opaque.

HONEY WALNUT SHRIMP

Servings: 4 | Prep: 15m | Cooks: 15m | Total: 30m

NUTRITION FACTS

Calories: 605.2 | Carbohydrates: 68g | Protein: 26.1g | Cholesterol: 179.4mg | Sodium: 340.2mg

INGREDIENTS

- 1 cup Water, municipal
- 2/3 cup Sugars, granulated
- 1/2 cup Nuts, walnuts, english
- 4 Egg, white, raw, fresh

- 1/4 cup Salad dressing, mayonnaise, soybean oil, with salt
- 1 pound Shrimp, fresh, raw, large (21-30)
- 2 tablespoons Honey, strained or extracted
- 1 tablespoon Milk, canned, condensed, sweetened

- 2/3 cup Rice flour, white
- 1 cup oil for frying

DIRECTIONS

1. Stir together the water and sugar in a small saucepan. Bring to a boil and add the walnuts. Boil for 2 minutes, then drain and place walnuts on a cookie sheet to dry.
2. Whip egg whites in a medium bowl until foamy. Stir in the mochiko until it has a pasty consistency. Heat the oil in a heavy deep skillet over medium-high heat. Dip shrimp into the mochiko batter, and then fry in the hot oil until golden brown, about 5 minutes. Remove with a slotted spoon and drain on paper towels.
3. In a medium serving bowl, stir together the mayonnaise, honey and sweetened condensed milk. Add shrimp and toss to coat with the sauce. Sprinkle the candied walnuts on top and serve.

SHRIMP AND FETA CHEESE PASTA

Servings: 5 | Prep: 15m | Cooks: 15m | Total: 30m

NUTRITION FACTS

Calories: 603.1 | Carbohydrates: 75.2g | Protein: 32.9g | Cholesterol: 168.2mg | Sodium: 763.3mg

INGREDIENTS

- 3 tablespoons Oil, olive, salad or cooking
- 1 pound Crustaceans, shrimp, mixed species, raw
- 5 cloves Garlic, raw
- 1 tablespoon Alcoholic beverage, wine, table, white
- 1 pound GG Linguine Pasta Semolina-Dry-5/8"Crcl QK
- 2 Tomatoes, red, ripe, raw
- 1 teaspoon Spices, oregano, ground
- 1/2 teaspoon Spices, basil, ground
- 1 (6 ounce) package Cheese, feta

DIRECTIONS

1. In a medium skillet over medium heat, heat 2 tablespoons olive oil. Cook shrimp, garlic and white wine for 5 minutes, or until shrimp is pink. Remove shrimp with slotted spoon and set aside.
2. Bring a large pot of lightly salted water to a boil. Add pasta and cook for 8 to 10 minutes or until al dente; drain.

3. While pasta is cooking, cook tomatoes with remaining 1 tablespoon oil, oregano and basil over medium heat in wine mixture until tender, 10 minutes.
4. Toss hot pasta with shrimp, tomato sauce and feta. Feta will melt slightly. Serve.

SEAFOOD ENCHILADAS

Servings: 6 | Prep: 15m | Cooks: 40m | Total: 55m

NUTRITION FACTS

Calories: 606.8 | Carbohydrates: 42.6g | Protein: 26.8g | Cholesterol: 135.8mg | Sodium: 1078mg

INGREDIENTS

- 1 Onions, raw
- 1 tablespoon Butter, with salt
- 1/2pound Crustaceans, crab, dungeness, raw
- 1/4 pound Crustaceans, shrimp, mixed species, raw
- 8 ounces Cheese, colby
- 6 (10 inch) flour tortilla (12 inch)

- 1 cup Cream, fluid, half and half
- 1/2cup Cream, sour, cultured
- 1/4 cup Butter, with salt
- 1 1/2teaspoons Spices, parsley, dried
- 1/2 teaspoon Garlic Salt GL 0130 HS

DIRECTIONS

1. Preheat oven to 350 degrees F (175 degrees C).
2. In a large skillet, saute onions in 1 tablespoon butter until transparent. Remove the skillet from heat and stir in crabmeat and shrimp. Shred the cheese and mix half of it into the seafood. Place a large spoonful of the mixture into each tortilla. Roll the tortillas up around the mixture and arrange the rolled tortillas in a 9x13 inch baking dish.
3. In a saucepan over medium-low heat, combine half-and-half, sour cream, 1/4 cup butter, parsley and garlic salt. Stir until the mixture is lukewarm and blended. Pour sauce over the enchiladas, and sprinkle with remaining cheese.
4. Bake in preheated oven for 30 minutes.

ANGEL HAIR PASTA WITH GARLIC SHRIMP AND BROCCOLI

Servings: 6 | Prep: 30m | Cooks: 30m | Total: 1h

NUTRITION FACTS

Calories: 430.7 | Carbohydrates: 39.5g | Protein: 24.3g | Cholesterol: 144.8mg | Sodium: 1139.3mg

INGREDIENTS

- 1 (12 ounce) package Di Giorno Angel Hair Pasta-Dry KFT
- 2 1/2tablespoons Butter, with salt
- 1 ½ tablespoons Wheat flour, white, all-purpose, enriched, bleached
- 1 1/2cups Milk, reduced fat, fluid, 2% milkfat, with added vitamin A
- 1/2cup Cream, fluid, heavy whipping
- 1 1/2tablespoons Pesto Sauce
- 1 1/2tablespoons Parsley, raw
- 3 cloves Garlic, raw
- 2 tablespoons Cheese, parmesan, grated
- 2 teaspoons Salt, table
- 1/2 teaspoon White Pepper-Ground-Dried FO
- 1 dash Worcestershire Sauce
- 1 dash Sauce, ready-to-serve, pepper or hot
- 1/2 (16 ounce) package Broccoli, frozen, chopped, unprepared
- 1 pound Crustaceans, shrimp, mixed species, raw
- 3 cloves Garlic, raw

DIRECTIONS

1. Bring a large pot of lightly salted water to a boil. Add pasta and cook for 8 to 10 minutes or until al dente; drain.
2. Melt 1.5 tablespoons butter in a medium saucepan over medium heat. Stir in flour and cook for 2 minutes. Slowly stir in milk and cream; simmer, stirring constantly, until thickened. Mix in pesto, parsley, 3 cloves minced garlic, Parmesan cheese, 1 teaspoon salt, white pepper, Worcestershire sauce and hot sauce. Reduce heat to low and allow to simmer.
3. Meanwhile, place broccoli in a steamer over 1 inch of boiling water, and cover. Cook until tender but still firm, about 2 to 6 minutes. Drain.
4. Melt 1 tablespoon butter in a large skillet. Saute shrimp, remaining 3 cloves minced garlic, and 1 teaspoon salt for 5 minutes, or until shrimp are pink.
5. In a large bowl, toss pasta, shrimp and broccoli; pour sauce over and serve.

DAVE'S LOW COUNTRY BOIL

Servings: 15 | Prep: 30m | Cooks: 30m | Total: 1h

NUTRITION FACTS

Calories: 722 | Carbohydrates: 45.8g | Protein: 67.6g | Cholesterol: 333.2mg | Sodium: 1575.9mg

INGREDIENTS

- 1 tablespoon Old Bay Seasoning TM
- 5 pounds new potatoes, raw; baby potatoes
- 3 (16 ounce) packages Kielbasa, kolbassy, pork, beef, nonfat dry milk added
- 8 ears Corn, sweet, yellow, raw
- 5 pounds Crustaceans, crab, dungeness, raw
- 4 pounds Crustaceans, shrimp, mixed species, raw

DIRECTIONS

1. Heat a large pot of water over an outdoor cooker, or medium-high heat indoors. Add Old Bay Seasoning to taste, and bring to a boil. Add potatoes, and sausage, and cook for about 10 minutes. Add the corn and crab; cook for another 5 minutes, then add the shrimp when everything else is almost done, and cook for another 3 or 4 minutes.
2. Drain off the water and pour the contents out onto a picnic table covered with newspaper. Grab a paper plate and a beer and enjoy!

SHRIMP FRIED RICE

Servings: 4 | Prep: 20m | Cooks: 10m | Total: 30m

NUTRITION FACTS

Calories: 483.4 | Carbohydrates: 60.3g | Protein: 20g | Cholesterol: 186.6mg | Sodium: 1637.6mg

INGREDIENTS

- 1 1/2 cups Rice, white, long-grain, regular, raw, enriched
- 3 cups Water, municipal
- 4 tablespoons Oil, soybean, salad or cooking
- 1 cup bean sprouts, fresh
- 1/4 cup Onions, spring or scallions (includes tops and bulb), raw
- 2 Egg, whole, raw, fresh
- 1 teaspoon Salt, table
- 1/4 teaspoon Spices, pepper, black

- 1/2 cup Onions, raw

- 1 1/2 cups Crustaceans, shrimp, mixed species, cooked, moist heat

- 4 tablespoons Soy sauce made from soy and wheat (shoyu)

- 1/4 teaspoon Oil, sesame, salad or cooking

DIRECTIONS

1. In a saucepan bring water to a boil. Add rice and stir. Reduce heat, cover and simmer for 20 minutes. Set aside and allow rice to cool.
2. Heat a large skillet or wok for 2 minutes. When the skillet or wok is hot, pour in vegetable oil, bean sprouts and onions. Mix well and cook for 3 minutes.
3. Mix in cooled rice and shrimp and cook for another 3 minutes. Stirring constantly.
4. Mix in green onions, eggs, salt, pepper, soy sauce and sesame oil. Cook for another 4 minutes, stirring continuously, until eggs are cooked and everything is blended evenly.

SESAME SHRIMP STIR-FRY

Servings: 4 | Prep: 15m | Cooks: 40m | Total: 55m

NUTRITION FACTS

Calories: 395 | Carbohydrates: 50.5g | Protein: 24.2g | Cholesterol: 172.9mg | Sodium: 885.3mg

INGREDIENTS

- 2 cups Water, municipal

- 1 cup Rice, white, long-grain, regular, raw, enriched

- 1 pound Crustaceans, shrimp, mixed species, raw

- 1/4teaspoon Spices, ginger, ground

- 1/4teaspoon Spices, pepper, red or cayenne

- 1 clove Garlic, raw

- 1 tablespoon Seeds, sesame seeds, whole, dried

- 1/4 teaspoon Spices, pepper, black

- 2 tablespoons Oil, sesame, salad or cooking

- 1 Peppers, sweet, red, raw; red bell pepper

- 3 Onions, spring or scallions (includes tops and bulb), raw

- 3 tablespoons Sauce, teriyaki, ready-to-serve

- 1/2 pound Bird's Eye Deluxe Sugar Snap Peas DFV

- 1/8 cup Cornstarch

- 3/4 cup Swanson Clear Chicken Broth CAM

- 1/4teaspoon Salt, table

DIRECTIONS

1. In a medium saucepan, bring salted water to a boil. Add rice, reduce heat, cover and simmer for 20 minutes.
2. While rice is simmering, combine shrimp, ginger, cayenne pepper, garlic, sesame seeds and black pepper in a large plastic food storage bag. Allow to marinate in the refrigerator.
3. Heat sesame oil in a large wok or skillet. Add red bell pepper and green onions; saute 3 to 4 minutes to soften slightly Add teriyaki sauce. Add peas and shrimp with seasoning; saute 4 minutes or until shrimp are opaque.
4. Stir cornstarch into chicken broth and add to wok; cook, stirring until mixture boils. Sprinkle with salt. Spoon shrimp mixture over rice.

SHRIMP ETOUFFEE

Servings: 4 | Prep: 35m | Cooks: 20m | Total: 1h15m

NUTRITION FACTS

Calories: 424 | Carbohydrates: 30.2g | Fat: 14.7g | Protein: 40.8g | Cholesterol: 369mg

Sodium: 1114mg

INGREDIENTS

- 3/4 teaspoon paprika
- 1/4 teaspoon ground thyme
- 1/4 teaspoon dried oregano
- 1/4 teaspoon cayenne pepper
- 1/4 teaspoon garlic powder
- 1/4 teaspoon onion powder
- 1/4 teaspoon white pepper
- 1/4 teaspoon ground black pepper
- 2 pounds shrimp, peeled and deveined
- 1/2 teaspoon salt
- 1 tablespoon vegetable oil

- 3 tablespoons butter
- 1/3 cup diced onion
- 1/3 cup diced green bell pepper
- 1/3 cup thinly sliced celery
- 2 tablespoons all-purpose flour, or as needed
- 1/2 cup diced tomatoes
- 1 3/4 cups chicken stock, or as needed
- 1/2 teaspoon Worcestershire sauce
- 1 dash hot sauce, or more to taste
- 1/4 cup sliced green onions
- 2 cups cooked rice, or to taste

DIRECTIONS

1. Whisk paprika, thyme, oregano, cayenne pepper, garlic powder, onion powder, white pepper, and black pepper together in a small bowl.
2. Drain shrimp in a colander for at least 15 minutes. Transfer to a bowl lined with paper towels and dry shrimp for about 3 minutes. Remove paper towels from bowl and season shrimp with 1 teaspoon salt and 1 teaspoon spice blend. Toss to coat shrimp with spice blend.
3. Heat vegetable oil a large heavy skillet over high heat until oil is smoking hot. Cook shrimp in the hot oil without stirring for 1 minute; stir, and cook 1 minute more.
4. Transfer shrimp to a large bowl. Let stand until juice forms in bowl. Strain shrimp juices into chicken stock to total 2 cups, adding more chicken stock if necessary.
5. Melt butter in large skillet over medium heat until butter begins to turn tan at the edges. Saute onion, celery, and green pepper in hot butter until softened, about 5 minutes. Pour in remaining spice blend.
6. Sprinkle flour into vegetable mixture and saute until combined, 3 to 4 minutes. Stir in tomatoes; cook until tomato juices begin to brown on bottom of pan, about 3 minutes. Whisk stock into vegetable mixture, stirring until smooth. Bring to a simmer and cook until slightly thickened and reduced to a gravy consistency, 3 to 5 minutes. Stir in Worcestershire sauce and hot sauce. Season with salt to taste.
7. Stir shrimp into etouffee sauce; let simmer until shrimp are cooked all the way through and no longer translucent, about 1 minute.
8. Garnish with green onions and a dusting of cayenne pepper. Pour over rice in large, shallow bowls.

ZIPPY SUMMER SHRIMP

Servings: 6 | Prep: 10m | Cooks: 10m | Total: 20m

NUTRITION FACTS

Calories: 238 | Carbohydrates: 2.2g | Protein: 25.1g | Cholesterol: 230.4mg | Sodium: 459.3mg

INGREDIENTS

- 1/3 cup Extra Virgin Olive Oil NOI
- 3 cloves Garlic, raw
- 1 teaspoon dried red pepper flakes
- 2 teaspoons Spices, paprika
- 2 pounds Shrimp, fresh, raw, jumbo (11-15)
- 1/4 cup Lemon juice, raw
- 2 tablespoons Basil, fresh
- 1/2 teaspoon Salt, table
- 1/4 teaspoon Spices, pepper, black

DIRECTIONS

1. Heat the oil in a large skillet over high heat; cook and stir the garlic in the oil until translucent. Sprinkle the red pepper flakes and paprika into the oil. Add the shrimp and toss to coat. Pour the lemon juice over the shrimp; allow to cook until the shrimp are bright pink on the outside and the

meat is no longer transparent in the center, 1 to 2 minutes more. Reduce heat to medium-low; add the basil and toss lightly. Season with salt and pepper to serve.

GARLIC SHRIMP SCAMPI

Servings: 4 | Prep: 5m | Cooks: 20m | Total: 25m

NUTRITION FACTS

Calories: 659.7 | Carbohydrates: 48.4g | Protein: 45.1g | Cholesterol: 323.1mg | Sodium: 737.4mg

INGREDIENTS

- 1 (8 ounce) package Di Giorno Angel Hair Pasta- Dry KFT
- 1/2 cup Butter, with salt
- 2 cloves Garlic, raw
- 1 1/2 pounds Crustaceans, shrimp, mixed species, raw
- 1/3 cup Burgundy Wine
- 3/4 cup Bread crumbs, dry, grated, plain
- 3 tablespoons Cheese, parmesan, grated

DIRECTIONS

1. Bring a large pot of salted water to a boil. Add angel hair pasta and return pot to boil. Cook until al dente. Drain well.
2. In a large saucepan, melt butter, saute garlic until tender, remove garlic and discard. Add shrimp and cook until colored pink. Stir in white wine. The bread crumbs are used as thickening, so stir in a little at a time until desired thickness is reached.
3. Serve shrimp over angel hair pasta, sprinkled with Parmesan cheese.

CREAMY CAJUN SHRIMP PASTA

Servings: 4 | Prep: 10m | Cooks: 10m | Total: 20m

NUTRITION FACTS

Calories: 483.3 | Carbohydrates: 46g | Protein: 34.4g | Cholesterol: 212.8mg | Sodium: 1271.5mg

INGREDIENTS

- 1 (8 ounce) package Di Giorno Angel Hair Pasta- Dry KFT
- 2 tablespoons Cajun Seasoning LF

- 1/4 cup Butter, with salt

- 1 pound Crustaceans, shrimp, mixed species, raw

- 1 clove Garlic, raw

- 1/4 cup Wheat flour, white, all-purpose, enriched, bleached

- 2 cups Milk, reduced fat, fluid, 2% milkfat, with added vitamin A

- 1/4 teaspoon Salt, table

- 1 tablespoon Lemon juice, raw

DIRECTIONS

1. Bring a large pot of lightly salted water to a boil. Add pasta and cook for 4 minutes or until al dente; drain.

2. Melt butter in a large heavy skillet over medium heat. Saute shrimp for 1 minute on each side. Stir in garlic, and cook for 1 minute. Remove shrimp with a slotted spoon; set aside. Stir in flour and Cajun seasoning. Cook, stirring for 5 minutes. Gradually whisk in milk, then cook until thickened. Remove from heat, and season with salt and lemon juice. Return shrimp to sauce, and spoon over cooked pasta.

SHRIMP LINGUINE ALFREDO

Servings: 4 | Prep: 10m | Cooks: 25m | Total: 35m

NUTRITION FACTS

Calories: 590.3 | Carbohydrates: 70.3g | Protein: 27.5g | Cholesterol: 135.5mg | Sodium: 316.9mg

INGREDIENTS

- 1 (12 ounce) package GG Linguine Pasta Semolina-Dry-5/8"Crcl QK

- 1/4 cup Butter, with salt

- 4 tablespoons Onions, raw

- 4 teaspoons Garlic, raw

- 40 small Crustaceans, shrimp, mixed species, raw

- 1 cup Cream, fluid, half and half

- 2 teaspoons Spices, pepper, black

- 6 tablespoons Cheese, parmesan, grated

- 4 sprigs Parsley, raw

- 4 slices Lemons, raw, with peel

DIRECTIONS

1. Cook pasta in a large pot of boiling water until al dente; drain.
2. Meanwhile, melt butter in a large saucepan. Saute onion and garlic over medium heat until tender. Add shrimp; saute over high heat for 1 minute, stirring constantly. Stir in half-and-half. Cook, stirring constantly, until sauce thickens.
3. Place pasta in a serving dish, and cover with shrimp sauce. Sprinkle with black pepper and Parmesan cheese. Garnish with parsley and lemon slices.

SEAFOOD CHOWDER

Servings: 8 | Prep: 15m | Cooks: 45m | Total: 1h

NUTRITION FACTS

Calories: 313.7 | Carbohydrates: 32g | Protein: 34.6g | Cholesterol: 157.8mg | Sodium: 1237.4mg

INGREDIENTS

- 1 1/2cups Milk, nonfat, fluid, with added vitamin A (fat free or skim)
- 1 (8 ounce) container Cheese, cream, fat free
- 2 cloves Garlic, raw
- 1 (26 ounce) can 98% Fat Free Cond Cream Mushroom Soup CAM
- 1 cup Onions, spring or scallions (includes tops and bulb), raw
- 1 cup Carrots, raw
- 1 (15.25 ounce) can Corn, sweet, yellow, canned, whole kernel, drained solids
- 1 1/2cups Potatoes, raw

- 1 teaspoon Spices, parsley, dried
- 1/2 teaspoon Spices, pepper, black
- 1/2 teaspoon Spices, pepper, red or cayenne
- 1/2pound Shrimp, fresh, raw, medium (31-35)
- 1/2
- 1/2pound Crustaceans, crab, dungeness, raw
- 1/2pound Squid, raw
- 1 (6.5 ounce) can Mollusks, clam, mixed species, canned, drained solids

DIRECTIONS

1. Place 1/2 cup milk, cream cheese, and garlic in a large pot over low heat. Cook and stir until blended. Mix in soup, green onions, carrots, corn with liquid, potatoes, parsley, and remaining milk. Season with black pepper and cayenne pepper. Simmer 25 minutes. Do not boil.
2. Mix the shrimp, scallops, crabmeat, calamari, and clams, and continue cooking 10 minutes, or until seafood is opaque.

LINGUINE PASTA WITH SHRIMP AND TOMATOES

Servings: 6 | Prep: 15m | Cooks: 40m | Total: 55m

NUTRITION FACTS

Calories: 520 | Carbohydrates: 61.5g | Fat: 16.1g | Protein: g | Cholesterol: 125mg | Sodium: 231mg

INGREDIENTS

- 2 tablespoons olive oil
- 3 cloves garlic, minced
- 4 cups diced tomatoes
- 1 cup dry white wine
- 2 tablespoons butter
- salt and black pepper to taste
- 1 (16 ounce) package linguine pasta
- 1 pound peeled and deveined medium shrimp
- 1 teaspoon Cajun seasoning
- 2 tablespoons olive oil

DIRECTIONS

1. Heat 2 tablespoons of olive oil in a large saucepan over medium heat. Stir in the garlic; cook 2 minutes. Add the tomatoes, and wine. Bring to a simmer and cook 30 minutes, stirring frequently. Once the tomatoes have simmered into a sauce, stir in the butter and season with salt and pepper.
2. Fill a large pot with lightly-salted water; bring to a rolling boil; stir in the linguine and return to a boil. Cook the pasta uncovered, stirring occasionally, until the pasta has cooked through but is still firm to the bite, about 11 minutes. Drain well in a colander set in the sink.
3. Season the shrimp with the Cajun seasoning, salt, and pepper. Heat the remaining 2 tablespoons of olive oil in a large skillet over medium-high heat. Stir in the shrimp and cook until pink on the outside and no longer translucent in the center, about 5 minutes. Stir the shrimp into the pasta sauce, then stir the sauce into the linguine to serve.

PESTO CREAM SAUCE

Servings: 8 | Prep: 30m | Cooks: 20m | Total: 50m

NUTRITION FACTS

Calories: 677.2 | Carbohydrates: 52.2g | Protein: 33.6g | Cholesterol: 154.9mg | Sodium: 738.2mg

INGREDIENTS

- 1 (16 ounce) package GG Linguine Pasta Semolina-Dry-5/8"Crcl QK
- 2 tablespoons Oil, olive, salad or cooking
- 1 small Onions, raw
- 8 cloves Garlic, raw
- 1/2 cup Butter, with salt
- 2 tablespoons Wheat flour, white, all-purpose, enriched, bleached
- 2 cups Milk, reduced fat, fluid, 2% milkfat, with added vitamin A

- 1 pinch Salt, table
- 1 pinch Spices, pepper, black
- 1 1/2 cups Cheese, pecorino romano
- 1 cup Pesto Sauce
- 1 pound Shrimp, fresh, frozen, medium (31-35)
- 20 Mushrooms, raw
- 3 roma (plum) tomato

DIRECTIONS

1. Bring a large pot of lightly salted water to a boil. Add pasta and cook for 8 to 10 minutes or until al dente; drain.
2. Heat olive oil in a large skillet over medium heat. Saute onion until tender and translucent. Stir in garlic and butter, and saute until garlic is soft and fragrant, about 1 minute. Dissolve flour in milk, then stir in. Season with salt and pepper, and simmer 4 minutes, stirring constantly. Add cheese, and stir until melted. Stir in pesto. Add shrimp, mushrooms and tomatoes. Cook 4 minutes, or until heated through. Toss with pasta until evenly coated.

MEXICAN SHRIMP COCKTAIL

Servings: 6 | Prep: 15m | Cooks: 0m | Total: 3h15m | Additional: 3h

NUTRITION FACTS

Calories: 257.8 | Carbohydrates: 15.8g | Protein: 33.3g | Cholesterol: 295.1mg | Sodium: 710.6mg

INGREDIENTS

- 2 pounds Crustaceans, shrimp, mixed species, medium, cooked, moist heat
- 1 tablespoon Garlic, raw
- 1/2 cup red onion
- 1/4cup Cilantro, raw
- 1 1/2 cups tomato and clam juice cocktail - USE ME
- 1/4cup Ketchup
- 1/4 cup Lime juice, raw
- 1 teaspoon Sauce, ready-to-serve, pepper, TABASCO
- 1/4cup Horseradish, prepared
- 1 pinch Salt, table
- 1 Avocados, raw, all commercial varieties

DIRECTIONS

1. Place the shrimp in a large bowl. Stir garlic, red onion, and cilantro. Mix in tomato and clam juice cocktail, ketchup, lime juice, hot pepper sauce, and horseradish. Season with salt. Gently stir in avocado. Cover, and refrigerate 2 to 3 hours. Serve in one large bowl or ladle into individual bowls.

LOUISIANA SHRIMP CREOLE

Servings: 5 | Prep: 20m | Cooks: 25m | Total: 45m

NUTRITION FACTS

Calories: 192.8 | Carbohydrates: 14.3g | Protein: g16.8 | Cholesterol: 156.6mg | Sodium: 677.3mg

INGREDIENTS

- 1/2 cup Onions, raw
- 1/2cup Peppers, sweet, green, raw; green bell pepper
- 1/2cup Celery, raw
- 2 cloves Garlic, raw
- 3 tablespoons Butter, with salt
- 1 (14.5 ounce) can Tomatoes, red, ripe, canned, stewed
- 1 (8 ounce) can Tomato products, canned, sauce
- 1 tablespoon Worcestershire Sauce
- 1 teaspoon Spices, chili powder
- 1 dash Sauce, ready-to-serve, pepper or hot

* 2 tablespoons Cornstarch
* 1 pound Crustaceans, shrimp, mixed species, raw

DIRECTIONS

1. In a 2 quart saucepan, melt butter or margarine over medium heat. Add onion, green pepper, celery, and garlic; cook until tender.
2. Mix in cornstarch. Stir in stewed tomatoes, tomato sauce, Worcestershire sauce, chili powder, and red pepper sauce. Bring to a boil, stirring frequently. Stir in shrimp, and cook for 5 minutes.

HONEY GRILLED SHRIMP

Servings: 3 | Prep: 30m | Cooks: 6m | Total: 1h36m | Additional: 1h

NUTRITION FACTS

Calories: 434.4 | Carbohydrates: 33.4g | Protein: 29.9g | Cholesterol: 279.5mg | Sodium: 1017.3mg

INGREDIENTS

* 1/2 teaspoon Spices, garlic powder
* 1/4tablespoon Spices, pepper, black
* 1/3 cup Worcestershire Sauce
* 2 tablespoons Burgundy Wine
* 2 tablespoons Salad dressing, italian, commercial, regular, with salt
* 1 pound Crustaceans, shrimp, mixed species, raw
* 1/4cup Honey, strained or extracted
* 1/4 cup Butter, with salt
* 2 tablespoons Worcestershire Sauce
* 3 eaches Skewers

DIRECTIONS

1. In a large bowl, mix together garlic powder, black pepper, 1/3 cup Worcestershire sauce, wine, and salad dressing; add shrimp, and toss to coat. Cover, and marinate in the refrigerator for 1 hour.
2. Preheat grill for high heat. Thread shrimp onto skewers, piercing once near the tail and once near the head. Discard marinade.
3. In a small bowl, stir together honey, melted butter, and remaining 2 tablespoons Worcestershire sauce. Set aside for basting.
4. Lightly oil grill grate. Grill shrimp for 2 to 3 minutes per side, or until opaque. Baste occasionally with the honey-butter sauce while grilling.

PENNE WITH SHRIMP

Servings: 8 | Prep: 10m | Cooks: 25m | Total: 35m

NUTRITION FACTS

Calories: 385.3 | Carbohydrates: 48.5g | Protein: 24.5g | Cholesterol: 95.1mg | Sodium: 398.5mg

INGREDIENTS

- 1 (16 ounce) package penne pasta, dry
- 2 tablespoons Oil, olive, salad or cooking
- 1/4 cup red onion
- 1 tablespoon Garlic, raw
- 1/4 cup Alcoholic beverage, wine, table, white
- 2 (14.5 ounce) cans S & W Ready Cut Tomatoes in Juice-Cnd-Cup SW
- 1 pound Shrimp, fresh, raw, medium (31-35)
- 1 cup Cheese, parmesan, grated

DIRECTIONS

1. Bring a large pot of lightly salted water to a boil. Add pasta and cook for 8 to 10 minutes or until al dente; drain.
2. Heat the oil in a skillet over medium heat. Stir in onion and garlic, and cook until onion is tender. Mix in wine and tomatoes, and continue cooking 10 minutes, stirring occasionally.
3. Mix shrimp into the skillet, and cook 5 minutes, or until opaque. Toss with pasta and top with Parmesan cheese to serve.

MARGARITA GRILLED SHRIMP

Servings: 4 | Prep: 15m | Cooks: 5m | Total: 50m

NUTRITION FACTS

Calories: 188 | Carbohydrates: 1.3g | Fat: 11.1g | Protein: 18.7g | Cholesterol: 173mg

INGREDIENTS

- 1 pound shrimp, peeled and deveined
- 3 tablespoons olive oil
- 3 tablespoons chopped fresh cilantro
- 2 teaspoons tequila
- 1/4 teaspoon cayenne pepper
- 1/4 teaspoon salt

* 2 tablespoons fresh lime juice
* 2 cloves garlic, minced
* 4 bamboo skewers, soaked in water for 20 minutes

DIRECTIONS

1. Stir shrimp, olive oil, cilantro, lime juice, garlic, tequila, cayenne pepper, and salt together in a bowl. Cover the bowl with plastic wrap and refrigerate shrimp in marinade for 30 minutes.
2. Preheat an outdoor grill for high heat and lightly oil grate.
3. Remove shrimp from bowl and thread onto skewers; discard marinade.
4. Cook on the preheated grill until shrimp turn pink, 2 to 3 minutes per side.

CHIPOTLE SHRIMP TACOS

Servings: 6 | Prep: 15m | Cooks: 15m | Total: 30m

NUTRITION FACTS

Calories: 377 | Carbohydrates: 26.2g | Fat: 11.1g | Protein: 41.9g | Cholesterol: 316mg | Sodium: 830mg

INGREDIENTS

* 1 (12 ounce) package bacon, cut into small pieces
* 1/2 onion, diced
* 2 pounds large cooked shrimp - peeled, deveined, and cut in half
* 3 chipotle peppers in adobo sauce, minced
* 12 corn tortillas
* 1 cup chopped fresh cilantro
* 1 lime, juiced
* salt to taste (optional)

DIRECTIONS

1. In a large, deep skillet fry the bacon over medium-high heat until evenly brown. Drain the bacon fat. Add the onions to the pan with the bacon and cook 5 minutes or until the onions are translucent. Stir in the shrimp and chipotle chiles; cook 4 minutes or until heated through.
2. Heat tortillas on an ungreased skillet over medium-high heat for 10 to 15 seconds. Turn and heat for another 5 to 10 seconds. Fill the heated tortillas with shrimp mixture. Sprinkle with cilantro, lime juice, and salt.

BUFFALO SHRIMP

Servings: 4 | Prep: 15m | Cooks: 20m | Total: 45m | Additional: 10m

NUTRITION FACTS

Calories: 625.7 | Carbohydrates: 54.4g | Protein: 30.1g | Cholesterol: 198.5mg | Sodium: 2128.8mg

INGREDIENTS

- 2 cups Wheat flour, white, all-purpose, enriched, bleached
- 2 tablespoons Creole-style seasoning
- 1 tablespoon Spices, garlic powder
- 1 tablespoon Spices, pepper, red or cayenne
- 1 teaspoon Spices, onion powder
- 1 teaspoon Spices, pepper, black
- 1 pound Crustaceans, shrimp, mixed species, raw
- 4 cups oil for frying
- 4 cloves Garlic, raw
- 2 1/2 tablespoons Butter, with salt
- 6 ounces Sauce, ready-to-serve, pepper or hot
- 1 teaspoon Spices, pepper, red or cayenne

DIRECTIONS

1. In a large resealable plastic bag, combine the flour, Creole-style seasoning, garlic powder, ground cayenne pepper, onion powder, and ground black pepper. Seal the bag and shake a few times to combine the ingredients well.
2. Rinse the shrimp under cold water and place them in the plastic bag with the flour mixture. Seal the bag and shake to coat all of the shrimp well with the flour mixture.
3. Place the coated shrimp on a cookie sheet and place in the refrigerator for 15 to 20 minutes. Save remaining flour mixture in the bag.
4. In a mixing bowl, whisk together garlic, butter hot sauce and cayenne pepper; set aside. In a pot, heat the oil to 375 degrees F (190 degrees C).
5. Remove shrimp from refrigerator and shake a second time in flour mixture.
6. Place the shrimp in hot oil and fry until pink, about 2 to 3 minutes. Immediately coat with buffalo sauce.

GRILLED GARLIC AND HERB SHRIMP

Servings: 4 | Prep: 10m | Cooks: 5m | Total: 2h15m | Additional: 2h

NUTRITION FACTS

Calories: 336.4 | Carbohydrates: 10.2g | Protein: 37.8g | Cholesterol: 345.6mg | Sodium: 400.8mg

INGREDIENTS

- 2 teaspoons Spices, paprika
- 2 tablespoons Garlic, raw
- 2 teaspoons Italian seasoning
- 2 tablespoons Lemon juice, raw
- 1/4 cup Oil, olive, salad or cooking
- 1/2 teaspoon Spices, pepper, black
- 2 teaspoons dried basil leaves
- 2 tablespoons Sugars, brown
- 2 pounds Shrimp, fresh, raw, large (21-30

DIRECTIONS

1. Whisk the paprika, garlic, Italian seasoning, lemon juice, olive oil, pepper, basil, and brown sugar together in a bowl until thoroughly blended. Stir in the shrimp, and toss to evenly coat with the marinade. Cover and refrigerate at least 2 hours, turning once.
2. Preheat an outdoor grill for medium-high heat. Lightly oil grill grate, and place about 4 inches from heat source.
3. Remove shrimp from marinade, drain excess, and discard marinade.
4. Place shrimp on preheated grill and cook, turning once, until opaque in the center, 5 to 6 minutes. Serve immediately.

ABSOLUTELY THE BEST SHRIMP SCAMPI

Servings: 4 | Prep: 20m | Cooks: 20m | Total: 40m

NUTRITION FACTS

Calories: 499.8 | Carbohydrates: 16g | Protein: 35.6g | Cholesterol: 268.7mg | Sodium: 532.4mg

INGREDIENTS

- 1/2cup Wheat flour, white, all-purpose, enriched, bleached
- 1/4 teaspoon Salt, table
- 1/2teaspoon Spices, pepper, black
- 1/4 teaspoon Spices, pepper, red or cayenne
- 1 1/2pounds Crustaceans, shrimp, mixed species, raw
- 4 cloves Garlic, raw
- 1 Shallots, raw
- 1/2 cup Parsley, raw
- 1/2teaspoon Pure Oregano-Whole-Dried FO
- 2 tablespoons Alcoholic beverage, wine, table, white

- 1/2cup Oil, olive, salad or cooking
- 2 tablespoons brandy, 100 proof

DIRECTIONS

1. In a small bowl, combine flour, salt, pepper and cayenne pepper. Mix thoroughly. Dredge shrimp in flour mixture.
2. In a large skillet, saute dredged shrimp in olive oil for 5 minutes over high heat. Toss shrimp often to prevent burning. Transfer shrimp with a slotted spoon to a serving dish, leaving the oil in the pan.
3. In the same pan, saute the garlic, shallot, parsley and oregano over medium heat for 3 minutes; stirring constantly. Spoon the mixture over the shrimp. Return pan to the heat. Preheat your broiler for medium heat.
4. Pour the wine and brandy into the skillet and ignite with a match or lighter. When the flames die down, stir to loosen any browned bits on the bottom of the skillet; pour over shrimp.
5. Place the serving dish of shrimp in a preheated broiler for about 2 minutes.

JAPANESE-STYLE DEEP-FRIED SHRIMP
Servings: 4 | Prep: 10m | Cooks: 10m | Total: 20m

NUTRITION FACTS

Calories: 630.1 | Carbohydrates: 53.7g | Protein: 28.3g | Cholesterol: 249.6mg | Sodium: 763.1mg

INGREDIENTS

- 1 pound Shrimp, fresh, raw, medium (31-35)
- 1/2 teaspoon Salt, table
- 1/2teaspoon Spices, pepper, black
- 1/2teaspoon Spices, garlic powder
- 1 cup Wheat flour, white, all-purpose, enriched, bleached
- 1 teaspoon Spices, paprika
- 2 Egg, whole, raw, fresh
- 1 cup Panko, bread crumbs
- 1 quart oil for frying

DIRECTIONS

1. Place the shrimp in a bowl and season with salt, pepper and garlic powder. In a small bowl, stir together the flour and paprika. Place eggs and panko crumbs into separate bowls.
2. Heat the oil in a deep-fryer or deep skillet to 375 degrees F (190 degrees C). Dip each shrimp into the flour mixture, then into the egg, and finally into the panko crumbs to coat. Fry a few at a time

until golden brown. This should take no longer than 5 minutes. Remove with a slotted spoon and drain on paper towels before serving.

ULTIMATE SHRIMP SCAMPI
Servings: 4 | Prep: 25m | Cooks: 15m | Total: 40m

NUTRITION FACTS

Calories: 791.9 | Carbohydrates: 72.6g | Protein: 36.1g | Cholesterol: 245.6mg | Sodium: 1345.4mg

INGREDIENTS

- 1 (16 ounce) package Di Giorno Angel Hair Pasta-Dry KFT
- 1/2cup Butter, with salt
- 4 cloves Garlic, raw
- 1/2cup Onions, raw
- 1 tablespoon Parsley, raw
- 1 teaspoon Salt, table
- 1/2teaspoon Spices, pepper, black
- 1 dash Worcestershire Sauce
- 1/4 cup Lemon juice, raw
- 1 teaspoon Alcoholic beverage, wine, table, white
- 1 pound Shrimp, fresh, raw, medium (31-35)
- 1/2 cup Asiago Cheese
- 1 large Avocados, raw, all commercial varieties

DIRECTIONS

1. Bring a large pot of lightly salted water to a boil over high heat. Add the angel hair pasta, and cook until al dente, 2 to 3 minutes; drain.
2. Melt the butter in a large skillet over medium heat. Stir in the garlic, onion, parsley, salt, pepper, Worcestershire sauce, lemon juice, and white wine. Once the mixture begins to bubble, increase the heat to medium-high, and stir in the shrimp. Cook and stir until the shrimp turn pink, and are no longer transparent in the center, about 5 minutes.
3. Serve the scampi over a bed of angel hair pasta, and sprinkle with Asiago cheese and avocado to serve.

LOW CARB JAMBALAYA

Servings: 6 | Prep: 15m | Cooks: 30m | Total: 45m

NUTRITION FACTS

Calories: 259.8 | Carbohydrates: 14.5g | Protein: 31.8g | Cholesterol: 166.6mg | Sodium: 974.5mg

INGREDIENTS

- 1 tablespoon Oil, olive, salad or cooking
- 1 tablespoon Butter, with salt
- 1 large Onions, raw
- 2 link (raw dimensions: 4" long x 7/8" dia), cookeds andouille sausage, pork and beef, cooked
- 6 cloves Garlic, raw
- 1 (14 ounce) can Tomatoes, crushed, canned
- 3 Peppers, sweet, green, raw; green bell pepper
- 2 Zucchini, raw
- 2 tablespoons Cajun Seasoning LF
- 1 teaspoon Sauce, ready-to-serve, pepper or hot
- 1 cup Swanson Clear Chicken Broth CAM
- 1 pound Chicken, broilers or fryers, breast, meat only, raw
- 1 pound Shrimp, fresh, raw, medium (31-35)

DIRECTIONS

1. Heat olive oil and butter in a large saucepan over medium heat. Add the onion and andouille sausage and cook and stir until the onion starts to brown, about 10 minutes. Stir in garlic and cook until fragrant, 1 to 2 minutes.
2. Mix in crushed tomatoes, green bell peppers, zucchinis, Cajun seasoning, hot sauce, and chicken broth; bring mixture to a boil, reduce to a simmer, and cook uncovered until the liquid cooks off and the mixture is thick, about 15 minutes. Stir in chicken and shrimp and simmer until heated through, 1 to 2 minutes.

BLACKENED SHRIMP STROGANOFF

Servings: 4 | Prep: 30m | Cooks: 30m | Total: 1h

NUTRITION FACTS

Calories: 440 | Carbohydrates: 41.4g | Fat: 16.1g | Protein: 33.1g | Cholesterol: 195mg

Sodium: 1208mg

INGREDIENTS

- 1 pound fresh shrimp, peeled and deveined
- 1 tablespoon olive oil
- 1 tablespoon Cajun seasoning
- 6 ounces fettuccini pasta
- 1 tablespoon butter
- 3 cups fresh mushrooms, sliced
- 1 tablespoon chopped shallots
- 2/3 cup chicken broth
- 1/2 cup sour cream
- 1 tablespoon cornstarch
- 1 cup chicken broth
- 1 (7 ounce) jar roasted red bell peppers
- 1 tablespoon drained capers

DIRECTIONS

1. Combine peeled shrimp, oil, and Cajun seasoning in a medium bowl. Set aside.
2. Bring a large pot of lightly salted water to a boil. Add pasta and cook for 8 to 10 minutes or until al dente; drain.
3. Meanwhile, melt butter over medium heat in a large frying pan. Cook and stir mushrooms and shallot in butter until tender. Remove from pan. Add shrimp cook until shrimp turn pink about 2 to 3 minutes. Remove from pan. Add 2/3 cup chicken broth to pan, and bring to a boil. Cook, uncovered, until reduced to 1/4 cup (2 to 3 minutes).
4. In a small bowl, stir together sour cream and cornstarch; mix in 1 cup chicken broth. Stir into reduced chicken broth in the frying pan. Cook and stir until thick and bubbly. Cook 1 minute more. Stir in shrimp, mushroom mixture, roasted red peppers, and capers. Heat through, and season to taste. Serve over pasta.

BAKED SEAFOOD AU GRATIN

Servings: 8 | Prep: 20m | Cooks: 1h | Total: 1h20m

NUTRITION FACTS

Calories: 565.8 | Carbohydrates: 20.4g | Protein: 42.8g | Cholesterol: 233.3mg | Sodium: 858.9mg

INGREDIENTS

- 1 Onions, raw
- 1 Peppers, sweet, green, raw; green bell pepper
- 1 cup Butter, with salt
- 1 cup Wheat flour, white, all-purpose, enriched, bleached
- 1 pound Crustaceans, crab, dungeness, raw
- 4 cups Water, municipal
- 1 pound Crustaceans, shrimp, mixed species, raw
- 1/2pound bay scallops, raw
- 1/2pound Finfish, flatfish (flounder and sole species), raw
- 3 cups Milk, reduced fat, fluid, 2% milkfat, with added vitamin A
- 1 cup Cheese, Cheddar, sharp
- 1 tablespoon Distilled Vinegar
- 1 teaspoon Worcestershire Sauce
- 1/2teaspoon Salt, table
- 1 pinch Spices, pepper, black
- 1 dash Sauce, ready-to-serve, pepper or hot
- 1/2 cup Cheese, parmesan, grated

DIRECTIONS

1. In a heavy skillet, saute the onion and the pepper in 1/2 cup of butter. Cook until tender. Mix in 1/2 cup of the flour, and cook over medium heat for 10 minutes, stirring frequently. Stir in crabmeat, remove from heat, and set aside.
2. In a large Dutch oven, bring the water to a boil. Add the shrimp, scallops, and flounder, and simmer for 3 minutes. Drain, reserving 1 cup of the cooking liquid, and set the seafood aside.
3. In a heavy saucepan, melt the remaining 1/2 cup butter over low heat. Stir in remaining 1/2 cup flour. Cook and stir constantly for 1 minute. Gradually add the milk plus the 1 cup reserved cooking liquid. Raise heat to medium; cook, stirring constantly, until the mixture is thickened and bubbly. Mix in the shredded Cheddar cheese, vinegar, Worcestershire sauce, salt, pepper, and hot sauce. Stir in cooked seafood.
4. Preheat oven to 350 degrees F (175 degrees C). Lightly grease one 9x13 inch baking dish. Press crabmeat mixture into the bottom of the prepared pan. Spoon the seafood mixture over the crabmeat crust, and sprinkle with the Parmesan cheese.
5. Bake in the preheated oven for 30 minutes, or until lightly browned. Serve immediately.

SHRIMP ETOUFFEE

Servings: 6 | Prep: 20m | Cooks: 25m | Total: 45m

NUTRITION FACTS

Calories: 194.8 | Carbohydrates: 9g | Protein: 14.8g | Cholesterol: 119.3mg | Sodium: 635.6mg

INGREDIENTS

- 1/4cup Margarine, regular, hard, corn (hydrogenated and regular)
- 1/2 cup Onions, raw
- 1/2cup Onions, spring or scallions (includes tops and bulb), raw
- 1/2cup Peppers, sweet, green, raw; green bell pepper
- 4 cloves Garlic, raw
- 1/2cup Celery, raw
- 1/2cup Parsley, raw
- 3 tablespoons Tomato products, canned, paste, with salt added
- 1 (10.75 ounce) can Soup, cream of chicken, canned, condensed, commercial
- 1 pound Crustaceans, shrimp, mixed species, raw
- Salt, table
- 1/4teaspoon Sauce, ready-to-serve, pepper or hot
- 1/4 teaspoon Spices, pepper, red or cayenne

DIRECTIONS

1. In a 2 quart microwave safe dish, combine margarine, onion, green onion, bell pepper, garlic and celery. Heat on High settings for 8 to 9 minutes.
2. Stir in parsley, tomato paste, soup, shrimp, salt, hot pepper sauce and cayenne. Heat on High setting for 5 minutes. Stir and cook for another 5 minutes until mixture thickens. Serve over white rice.

BIG ED'S CAJUN SHRIMP SOUP

Servings: 6 | Prep: 15m | Cooks: 25m | Total: 40m

NUTRITION FACTS

Calories: 162.5 | Carbohydrates: 19.6g | Protein: 13.8g | Cholesterol: 92.5mg | Sodium: 722.3mg

INGREDIENTS

- 1 tablespoon Butter, with salt
- 1/2cup Peppers, sweet, green, raw; green bell pepper
- 1/4cup Onions, spring or scallions (includes tops and bulb), raw
- 1 clove Garlic, raw
- 3 cups Vegetable juice cocktail, canned
- 1 (8 ounce) bottle Mollusks, clam, mixed species, canned, liquid
- 1/2cup Water, municipal
- 1/4teaspoon Spices, thyme, dried
- 1/4 teaspoon dried basil leaves
- 1/4 teaspoon dried red pepper flakes
- 1 Spices, bay leaf, crumbled
- 1/2teaspoon Salt, table
- 1/2 cup Rice, white, long-grain, regular, raw, enriched
- 3/4 pound Crustaceans, shrimp, mixed species, raw
- 1 teaspoon Sauce, ready-to-serve, pepper or hot

DIRECTIONS

1. Melt butter in a large pot over medium heat. Saute green bell pepper, onions, and garlic until tender. Stir in vegetable juice, clam juice, and water. Season with thyme, basil, red pepper, bay leaf, and salt. Bring to a boil, and stir in rice. Reduce heat, and cover. Simmer 15 minutes, until rice is tender.
2. Stir in shrimp, and cook 5 minutes, or until shrimp are opaque. Remove the bay leaf, and season with hot sauce.

SHRIMP AND GRITS

Servings: 4 | Prep: 25m | Cooks: 30m | Total: 55m

NUTRITION FACTS

Calories: 434 | Carbohydrates: 33.2g | Fat: 19.5g | Protein: 30.1g | Cholesterol: 226mg

Sodium: 1498mg

INGREDIENTS

- 4 slices bacon, cut into 1/4-inch pieces
- 1/4 cup water
- 1 pound shrimp, peeled and deveined
- 1/2 teaspoon Cajun seasoning

- 2 tablespoons heavy whipping cream
- 2 teaspoons lemon juice
- 1 dash Worcestershire sauce
- 4 cups water
- 2 tablespoons butter
- 1 teaspoon salt
- 1 cup white grits
- 1/2 cup shredded white Cheddar cheese
- 1/2 teaspoon salt, or to taste
- 1/4 teaspoon ground black pepper
- 1 pinch cayenne pepper
- 1 tablespoon minced jalapeno pepper
- 2 tablespoons minced green onion
- 3 cloves garlic, minced
- 1 tablespoon chopped fresh parsley

DIRECTIONS

1. Place bacon in a large skillet and cook over medium-high heat, turning occasionally, until almost crisp, 5 to 7 minutes. Remove from heat and transfer bacon to a dish, leaving drippings in the skillet.
2. Whisk 1/4 cup water, cream, lemon juice, and Worcestershire sauce together in a bowl.
3. Stir 4 cups water, butter, and 1 teaspoon salt together in a pot; bring to a boil. Whisk grits into pot, bring to a simmer, reduce heat to low, and cook until grits are creamy, 20 to 25 minutes. Remove from heat and stir white Cheddar cheese into grits.
4. Place shrimp in a large bowl and season with Cajun seasoning, 1/2 teaspoon salt, black pepper, and a pinch of cayenne pepper.
5. Heat skillet with bacon drippings over high heat. Cook shrimp in hot bacon fat in a single layer for 1 minute. Turn shrimp and add jalapeno; cook until fragrant, about 30 seconds. Stir cream mixture, bacon, green onion, and garlic to shrimp mixture; cook and stir, adding water as necessary to thin the sauce, until shrimp are cooked through, 3 to 4 minutes. Remove from heat and stir in parsley.
6. Ladle grits into a bowl and top with shrimp and sauce.

SHRIMP AND CRAB ENCHILADAS

Servings: 12 | Prep: 15m | Cooks: 45m | Total: 1h

NUTRITION FACTS

Calories: 570.8 | Carbohydrates: 65g | Protein: 26.8g | Cholesterol: 120.1mg | Sodium: 995.8mg

INGREDIENTS

- 12 (12 inch) flour tortilla (12 inch)
- 8 ounces Cheese, monterey
- 1 (20 ounce) can Green Enchilada Sauce
- 1 (8 ounce) container Cream, sour, cultured

- 1 (6 ounce) can Crab, canned
- 1 pound Crustaceans, shrimp, mixed species, medium, cooked, moist heat
- 1 bunch Onions, spring or scallions (includes tops and bulb), raw

DIRECTIONS

1. Preheat oven to 350 degrees F (175 degrees C).
2. Lay tortillas on a flat surface. In the middle of each tortilla place equal amounts of cheese, crab, and shrimp. Set aside some cheese to sprinkle on top of the tortillas. Roll the tortillas to form enchiladas. Arrange side by side in a 9x13 inch baking pan.
3. Pour green enchilada sauce over all of the enchiladas; the green sauce should cover the enchiladas completely. Sprinkle the remaining cheese over the enchiladas.
4. Cover, and bake for 30 minutes in the preheated oven. Remove cover, and continue baking 15 minutes. Top enchiladas with sour cream and green onions to serve.

AWESOME EGG ROLLS

Servings: 8 | Prep: 30m | Cooks: 15m | Total: 45m

NUTRITION FACTS

Calories: 207.8 | Carbohydrates: 17.7g | Protein: 7.2g | Cholesterol: 49.3mg | Sodium: 395.9mg

INGREDIENTS

- 6 cups Cabbage, raw
- 1 Carrots, raw
- 1/2 cup bean sprouts, fresh
- 1 Celery, raw
- 2 tablespoons Onions, raw
- 1 (4 ounce) can Crustaceans, shrimp, mixed species, canned
- 2 tablespoons Soy sauce made from soy and wheat (shoyu)
- 1/8 teaspoon Spices, garlic powder
- 1 pinch Spices, pepper, black
- 1 Egg, whole, raw, fresh
- 1 tablespoon Cornstarch
- 20 eaches Wonton wrappers (includes egg roll wrappers)
- 1 quart oil for frying

DIRECTIONS

1. In a large bowl, mix together cabbage, carrots, sprouts, celery, and onion. Stir in shrimp, soy sauce, garlic powder, and black pepper.
2. Pour beaten egg into a skillet placed over medium heat; cook flat and thin, flipping once, until done. Remove from skillet, cool, and chop finely. Stir egg into cabbage mixture. Sprinkle top with cornstarch, mix, and allow to sit 10 minutes.
3. Mix 1 tablespoon cornstarch with 2 tablespoons cold water. Set aside.
4. Place 2 or 3 tablespoons of the shrimp mixture into the center of an egg roll skin. Dip a spoon into the water and cornstarch mixture, and moisten all corners but the bottom corner. Fold the egg roll skin from the bottom over the mixture, making a tight tube of the shrimp mixture. Fold corners in from the sides, and press to stick against folded roll. Then roll the rest of the way. Repeat with remaining egg roll wrappers.
5. Pour vegetable oil into a deep frying pan to a depth of 3 or 4 inches, and heat oil to 350 degrees F (175 degrees C). Carefully place egg rolls into hot oil, and fry until golden brown. Remove to paper towels.

INDIAN SHRIMP CURRY

Servings: 4 | Prep: 15m | Cooks: 15m | Total: 30m

NUTRITION FACTS

Calories: 416.2 | Carbohydrates: 10.9g | Protein: 23g | Cholesterol: 146mg | Sodium: 930.4mg

INGREDIENTS

- 2 tablespoons Oil, peanut, salad or cooking
- 1/2 sweet onion
- 2 cloves Garlic, raw
- 1 teaspoon Spices, ginger, ground
- 1 teaspoon cumin, ground
- 1 1/2 teaspoons Spices, turmeric, ground
- 1 teaspoon Spices, paprika
- 1/2 teaspoon Spices, chili powder
- 1 (14.5 ounce) can S & W Ready Cut Tomatoes in Juice-Cnd-Cup SW
- 1 (14 ounce) can Nuts, coconut milk, canned (liquid expressed from grated meat and water)
- 1 teaspoon Salt, table
- 1 pound Shrimp-Ckd FDA
- 2 tablespoons Cilantro, raw

DIRECTIONS

1. Heat the oil in a large skillet over medium heat; cook the onion in the hot oil until translucent, about 5 minutes. Remove the skillet from the heat and allow it to cool slightly, about 2 minutes. Add the garlic, ginger, cumin, turmeric, paprika, and ground chile (see Note) to the onion and stir over low heat. Pour the tomatoes and coconut milk into the skillet; season with salt.
2. Cook the mixture at a simmer, stirring occasionally, about 10 minutes. Stir the shrimp, fresh cilantro, and dried cilantro into the sauce mixture; cook another 1 minute before serving.

SPICY LIME GRILLED SHRIMP

Servings: 8 | Prep: 5m | Cooks: 5m | Total: 30m | Additional: 20m

NUTRITION FACTS

Calories: 68.6 | Carbohydrates: 2.2g | Protein: 9.5g | Cholesterol: 86.3mg | Sodium: 632.5mg

INGREDIENTS

- 3 tablespoons Cajun Seasoning LF
- 1 tablespoon Oil, soybean, salad or cooking
- 1 Limes, raw
- 1 pound Shrimp, fresh, raw, medium (31-35)

DIRECTIONS

1. Mix together the Cajun seasoning, lime juice, and vegetable oil in a resealable plastic bag. Add the shrimp, coat with the marinade, squeeze out excess air, and seal the bag. Marinate in the refrigerator for 20 minutes.
2. Preheat an outdoor grill for medium heat, and lightly oil the grate. Remove the shrimp from the marinade, and shake off excess. Discard the remaining marinade.
3. Cook the shrimp on the preheated grill until they are bright pink on the outside and the meat is no longer transparent in the center, about 2 minutes per side.

THAI SPICED BARBECUE SHRIMP

Servings: 8 | Prep: 1h | Cooks: 6m | Total: 1h6m

NUTRITION FACTS

Calories: 73 | Carbohydrates: 3.6g | Protein: 11.7g | Cholesterol: 86.3mg | Sodium: 268.3mg

INGREDIENTS

- 3 tablespoons Lemon juice, raw
- 1 tablespoon Sugars, brown

- 1 tablespoon Soy sauce made from soy and wheat (shoyu)
- 1 tablespoon Dijon Mustard NB
- 2 cloves Garlic, raw
- 2 teaspoons curry paste
- 1 pound Shrimp, fresh, raw, medium (31-35)

DIRECTIONS

1. In a shallow dish or resealable bag, mix together the lemon juice, soy sauce, mustard, garlic, brown sugar and curry paste. Add shrimp, and seal or cover. Marinate in the refrigerator for 1 hour.
2. Preheat a grill for high heat. When the grill is hot, lightly oil the grate. Thread the shrimp onto skewers, or place in a grill basket for easy handling. Transfer the marinade to a saucepan, and boil for a few minutes.
3. Grill shrimp for 3 minutes per side, or until opaque. Baste occasionally with the marinade.

FRESH TOMATO SHRIMP PASTA

Servings: 4 | Prep: 15m | Cooks: 15m | Total: 30m

NUTRITION FACTS

Calories: 651 | Carbohydrates: 52.2g | Protein: 43.8g | Cholesterol: 265.9mg | Sodium: 357.5mg

INGREDIENTS

- 8 ounces GG Fettucine Pasta Semol-Dry-3/8"Crcl QK
- 3 cloves Garlic, raw
- 1/2 sweet onion
- 3 tablespoons Fresh Oregano
- 4 tablespoons Oil, olive, salad or cooking
- 4 medium Tomatoes, red, ripe, raw
- 3 tablespoons Basil, fresh
- 1 pinch Salt, table
- 1 cup Spinach, raw
- 1 pound Crustaceans, shrimp, mixed species, cooked, moist heat
- 8 ounces Fresh Mozzarella Cheese BC

DIRECTIONS

1. Bring a large pot of lightly salted water to a boil. Add the pasta, and cook for 8 minutes, or until tender. Drain.

2. In the container of a food processor, combine the garlic, onion and oregano. Pulse until finely chopped. Heat the olive oil in a large skillet over medium heat. Add the onion mixture; cook and stir until fragrant and almost golden. Mix in the tomatoes, basil, salt and pepper. Simmer for about 5 minutes while the pasta is cooking, stirring occasionally.

3. Mix in spinach until it wilts, then just before the pasta is done, stir in the shrimp. Cook until heated through. Toss with pasta in a large serving bowl, and mix in mozzarella cheese.

BAKED FISH WITH SHRIMP

Servings: 5 | Prep: 5m | Cooks: 40m | Total: 45m

NUTRITION FACTS

Calories: 340.6 | Carbohydrates: 4.8g | Protein: 50.3g | Cholesterol: 180.9mg | Sodium: 545.4mg

INGREDIENTS

- 3 tablespoons Butter, with salt
- 2 tablespoons Wheat flour, white, all-purpose, enriched, bleached
- 1/2 teaspoon Salt, table
- 1 cup Milk, reduced fat, fluid, 2% milkfat, with added vitamin A

- 2 pounds Finfish, snapper, mixed species, raw
- 1/2 pound Crustaceans, shrimp, mixed species, cooked, moist heat
- 1/4 cup Cheese, parmesan, grated

DIRECTIONS

1. Preheat oven to 325 degrees F (165 degrees C).
2. In a small saucepan, melt butter over medium low heat. Whisk in flour and salt to make a paste. Gradually whisk in milk. Stirring constantly, cook until sauce is thick enough to coat the back of a spoon.
3. Select a pan large enough to accommodate all the fillets in one layer. Coat with cooking spray. Arrange fish in pan, and cover with shrimp.. Pour white sauce over shrimp. Sprinkle with grated cheese.
4. Bake, uncovered, for 20 to 25 minutes.

AMAZING SPICY GRILLED SHRIMP

Servings: 6 | Prep: 40m | Cooks: 4m | Total: 2h44m | Additional: 2h

NUTRITION FACTS

Calories: 320 | Carbohydrates: 4.1g | Protein: 25.1g | Cholesterol: 230.4mg | Sodium: 827.3mg

INGREDIENTS

- 1/3 cup Oil, olive, salad or cooking
- 1/4 cup Oil, sesame, salad or cooking
- 1/4 cup Parsley, raw
- 2 tablespoons Sauce, ready-to-serve, pepper or hot
- 2 tablespoons Garlic, raw
- 1 tablespoon Ketchup
- 1 tablespoon chili paste
- 1 teaspoon Salt, table
- 1 teaspoon Spices, pepper, black
- 3 tablespoons Lemon juice, raw
- 2 pounds Shrimp, fresh, raw, large (21-30)
- 12 eaches Skewers

DIRECTIONS

1. Whisk together the olive oil, sesame oil, parsley, hot sauce, minced garlic, ketchup, chile sauce, salt, pepper, and lemon juice in a mixing bowl. Set aside about 1/3 of this marinade to use while grilling.
2. Place the shrimp in a large, resealable plastic bag. Pour in the remaining marinade and seal the bag. Refrigerate for 2 hours.
3. Preheat an outdoor grill for high heat. Thread shrimp onto skewers, piercing once near the tail and once near the head. Discard marinade.
4. Lightly oil grill grate. Cook shrimp for 2 minutes per side until opaque, basting frequently with reserved marinade.

AVOCADO SHRIMP CEVICHE-ESTILLO SARITA

Servings: 4 | Prep: 1h30m | Cooks: 0m | Total: 1h30m

NUTRITION FACTS

Calories: 352.1 | Carbohydrates: 24.3g | Protein: 40.5g | Cholesterol: 345.6mg | Sodium: 690.7mg

INGREDIENTS

- 2 pounds Shrimp, fresh, raw, large (21-30)
- 1 tablespoon Ketchup

- 3/4 cup Lime juice, raw
- 5 roma (plum) tomato
- 1 white onion, raw
- 1/2 cup Cilantro, raw
- 1 tablespoon Worcestershire Sauce
- 1 teaspoon Sauce, ready-to-serve, pepper or hot
- 1 pinch Salt, table
- 1 Avocados, raw, all commercial varieties
- 16 Crackers, saltines (includes oyster, soda, soup)

DIRECTIONS

1. Place the shrimp and lime juice into a large bowl, and stir to coat. Let stand for about 5 minutes, or until shrimp are opaque. The lime juice will cook them. Mix in the tomatoes, onion, and cilantro until coated with lime juice; cover and refrigerate for 1 hour.
2. Remove from the refrigerator, and mix in the Worcestershire sauce, ketchup, hot sauce, salt and pepper. We have our own hot sauce recipe, but you can use whatever hot sauce you like, or leave it out and let people add their own when serving.
3. Serve in glass tumblers and top with avocado pieces. Set out extra Worcestershire sauce, ketchup, lime wedges and hot sauce for people to individualize their dish. Serve with saltine crackers.

FIRE ROASTED TOMATO AND FETA PASTA WITH SHRIMP

Servings: 2 | Prep: 15m | Cooks: 12m | Total: 27m

NUTRITION FACTS

Calories: 702 | Carbohydrates: 94.8g | Fat: 23.4g | Protein: 31.8g | Cholesterol: 111mg

Sodium: 1354mg

INGREDIENTS

- 1/2 pound linguine pasta
- 1 tablespoon olive oil
- 3 cloves garlic, minced
- 12 medium shrimp, peeled and deveined
- 1 (14.5 ounce) can fire roasted tomatoes
- 1 tablespoon chopped fresh basil
- salt and pepper to taste
- 1/2 cup crumbled feta cheese

DIRECTIONS

1. Bring a large pot of lightly salted water to a boil. Add pasta and cook for 8 to 10 minutes or until al dente; drain.
2. While the pasta is cooking, heat the olive oil in a large skillet over medium heat. Add the garlic; cook and stir until fragrant, about 1 minute. Add the shrimp, and cook until opaque, about 3 to 5 minutes. Pour in the tomatoes and heat through. Season with basil, salt and pepper.
3. Toss the cooked pasta in the sauce, and sprinkle with crumbled feta to serve.

HONEY GINGER SHRIMP

Servings: 4 | Prep: 10m | Cooks: 10m | Total: 20m

NUTRITION FACTS

Calories: 165.9 | Carbohydrates: 4.1g | Protein: 19g | Cholesterol: 172.9mg | Sodium: 199.9mg

INGREDIENTS

- 2 tablespoons Oil, olive, salad or cooking
- 1 tablespoon dried red pepper flakes
- 1 teaspoon Garlic, raw
- 1/4 Onions, raw
- 1 teaspoon Spices, ginger, ground
- 1 teaspoon Honey, strained or extracted
- 1 pound Shrimp, fresh, raw, medium (31-35)
- 1 pinch Salt, table

DIRECTIONS

1. Heat the olive oil and red pepper flakes in a large skillet over medium heat. Add the onions, garlic, ginger and honey; cook and stir until fragrant. Add the shrimp, and cook for 5 minutes, stirring as needed, until shrimp are pink and opaque. Serve immediately.

THAI CURRY SOUP

Servings: 4 | Prep: 15m | Cooks: 35m | Total: 50m

NUTRITION FACTS

Calories: 246.6 | Carbohydrates: 23.8g | Protein: 8.2g | Cholesterol: 30mg | Sodium: 1694.7mg

INGREDIENTS

- 2 ounces Rice noodles, dry
- 1 tablespoon Sugars, granulated

- 1 tablespoon Oil, olive, salad or cooking
- 1 clove Garlic, raw
- 1 1/2 tablespoons Lemon grass (citronella), raw
- 1 teaspoon Spices, ginger, ground
- 2 teaspoons curry paste
- 1 (32 ounce) carton Swanson Clear Chicken Broth CAM
- 2 tablespoons Soy sauce made from soy and wheat (shoyu)
- 1 (13.5 ounce) can light coconut milk
- 1/2 cup Shrimp, fresh, raw, medium (31-35)
- 1/2 cup Mushrooms, raw
- 1 (10 ounce) bag Spinach, raw
- 2 tablespoons Lime juice, raw
- 1/4 cup Cilantro, raw
- 2 eaches Onions, spring or scallions

DIRECTIONS

1. Bring a large pot of lightly salted water to a boil. Add rice noodles and cook until al dente, about 3 minutes. Drain and rinse well with cold water to stop the cooking; set aside.
2. Heat oil in a large saucepan over medium heat. Stir in garlic, lemon grass, and ginger; cook and stir until aromatic, 30 to 60 seconds. Add the curry paste, and cook 30 seconds more. Pour in about 1/2 cup of the chicken broth, and stir until the curry paste has dissolved, then pour in the remaining chicken stock along with the soy sauce and sugar. Bring to a boil, then reduce heat to medium-low, partially cover, and simmer 20 minutes.
3. Stir in coconut milk, shrimp, mushrooms, spinach, lime juice, and cilantro. Increase heat to medium-high, and simmer until the shrimp turn pink and are no longer translucent, about 5 minutes.
4. To serve, place some rice noodles into each serving bowl and ladle soup on top of them. Garnish each bowl with a sprinkle of sliced green onion.

CREAMY SHRIMP AND CRAB BISQUE

Servings: 6 | Prep: 5m | Cooks: 15m | Total: 20m

NUTRITION FACTS

Calories: 218.5 | Carbohydrates: 5.9g | Protein: 17.2g | Cholesterol: 110.2mg | Sodium: 770.6mg

INGREDIENTS

- 2 tablespoons Butter, with salt
- 2 tablespoons Wheat flour, white, all-purpose, enriched, bleached
- 2 tablespoons Onions, raw
- 1 1/2 cups Cream, fluid, half and half

- 1/2teaspoon Salt, table

- 1/4 teaspoon Spices, pepper, white

- 1 teaspoon Soup, chicken broth or bouillon, dehydrated, dry

- 1/2pound Crustaceans, shrimp, mixed species, raw

- 1/2pound Crustaceans, crab, alaska king, cooked, moist heat

- 1/2 cup Alcoholic beverage, wine, table, white

DIRECTIONS

1. In a large saucepan, melt butter over a low heat. Stir in flour, salt, white pepper, bouillon granules, and onion. Blend 3/4 cup half-and-half cream into the mixture. Mix in shrimp and crab meat. Turn the temperature to medium heat and continue stirring until the mixture thickens.
2. Blend the remaining half-and-half cream and wine into the mixture. Serve and enjoy.

REMOULADE SAUCE A LA NEW ORLEANS

Servings: 6 | Prep: 20m | Cooks: 0m | Total: 20m

NUTRITION FACTS

Calories: 359 | Carbohydrates: 6.7g | Protein: 1g | Cholesterol: 13.9mg | Sodium: 942.7mg

INGREDIENTS

- 1 cup Salad dressing, mayonnaise, soybean oil, with salt
- 1/4 cup Tomato Base Chili Sauce
- 2 tablespoons Creole honey mustard
- 2 tablespoons Extra Virgin Olive Oil NOI
- 1 tablespoon Sauce, ready-to-serve, pepper or hot
- 2 tablespoons Lemon juice, raw
- 1 teaspoon Worcestershire Sauce
- 4 medium Onions, spring or scallions (includes tops and bulb), raw

- 2 tablespoons Parsley, raw

- 2 tablespoons Olives, green, pitted

- 2 tablespoons Celery, raw

- 1 clove Garlic, raw

- 1/2teaspoon Spices, chili powder

- 1 teaspoon Salt, table

- 1/2 teaspoon Spices, pepper, black

- 1 teaspoon Capers, canned

DIRECTIONS

1. Mix together mayonnaise, chili sauce, mustard, olive oil, hot sauce, lemon juice, and Worcestershire sauce. Stir in scallions, parsley, olives, celery, capers, and garlic. Season with chili powder, and salt and pepper. Cover, and refrigerate.

SHRIMP FLORENTINE WITH ZOODLES

Servings: 4 | Prep: 10m | Cooks: 15m | Total: 25m

NUTRITION FACTS

Calories: 229.2 | Carbohydrates: 7.1g | Protein: 21g | Cholesterol: 195.5mg | Sodium: 780.7mg

INGREDIENTS

- 1 tablespoon Butter, with salt
- 1 tablespoon Extra Virgin Olive Oil NOI
- 2 eaches Zucchini, raw
- 1/2large Onions, raw
- 1 tablespoon Garlic, raw
- 1/2teaspoon Morton Kosher Salt, coarse
- 2 tablespoons Butter, with salt
- 1 pound Shrimp, fresh, raw, large (21-30)
- 1 teaspoon Garlic, raw
- 1 (6 ounce) bag Spinach, raw
- 1 tablespoon Lemon juice, raw
- 1 teaspoon dried red pepper flakes
- 1/2 teaspoon Morton Kosher Salt, coarse
- 1/2teaspoon Spices, pepper, black

DIRECTIONS

1. Heat 1 tablespoon butter and olive oil together in a large skillet over medium heat; cook and stir zucchini noodles (zoodles), onion, chopped garlic, and 1/2 teaspoon salt until zoodles are tender and onion is translucent, about 5 minutes. Transfer zoodle mixture to a bowl.
2. Heat 2 tablespoons butter in the same skillet; cook and stir shrimp and minced garlic until shrimp are just pink, 3 to 4 minutes. Add spinach, lemon juice, red pepper flakes, 1/2 teaspoon salt, and pepper; cook and stir until spinach begins to wilt, 3 to 4 minutes. Add zoodle mixture; cook and stir until heated through, 2 to 3 minutes.

SPICY GARLIC AND PEPPER SHRIMP

Servings: 1 | Prep: 25m | Cooks: 10m | Total: 35m

NUTRITION FACTS

Calories: 405.8 | Carbohydrates: 12.1g | Protein: 12.3g | Cholesterol: 85.3mg | Sodium: 1017.1mg

INGREDIENTS

- 2 1/2 tablespoons Oil, vegetable corn, salad or cooking
- 1/4 cup Water, municipal
- 1 cup Cabbage, raw
- 1 tablespoon Garlic, raw
- 8 large Crustaceans, shrimp, mixed species, raw
- 2 teaspoons Spices, pepper, red or cayenne
- 2 tablespoons Onions, raw
- 1 tablespoon Cilantro, raw
- 1 tablespoon Soy sauce made from soy and wheat (shoyu)

DIRECTIONS

1. Heat 1 tablespoon oil in a skillet over high heat. Add cabbage and 1 tablespoon water stir-fry for 30 seconds. Remove cabbage from skillet and place on a serving platter.
2. Heat the remaining 1 1/2 tablespoons oil in the skillet over high heat. Place the garlic and shrimp in the skillet and stir until garlic is lightly browned and shrimp turns pink. Add pepper, onion, cilantro, soy sauce and remaining water to the skillet. Stir-fry for 10 seconds. Pour the hot mixture onto the cabbage.

ANN'S SHRIMP ETOUFFEE

Servings: 20 | Prep: 30m | Cooks: 1h40m | Total: 2h25m | Additional: 15m

NUTRITION FACTS

Calories: 204.9 | Carbohydrates: 3.9g | Protein: 22.9g | Cholesterol: 203.7mg | Sodium: 328mg

INGREDIENTS

- 1 cup Butter, with salt
- 2 large white onion, raw
- 1 cup Mushrooms, raw
- 3 tablespoons Spices, paprika

- 6 stalks Celery, raw
- 3 cloves Garlic, raw
- 4 tablespoons Wheat flour, white, all-purpose, enriched, bleached
- 5 pounds Crustaceans, shrimp, mixed species, raw
- Salt, table
- Spices, pepper, black
- dried red pepper flakes

DIRECTIONS

1. In a large skillet, melt butter and saute onions, celery and garlic for about 45 minutes or until they are cooked down.
2. Stir in flour and cook briefly, do not brown. Stir in chopped shrimp and cook for 20 minutes.
3. Pour in 2 to 3 cups of water and mushrooms. Stir in paprika and season with salt, pepper and red pepper flakes. Cook for 30 minutes. Should be a thick and have a gravy-like consistency.

CURRY-COCONUT SHRIMP

Servings: 4 | Prep: 10m | Cooks: 25m | Total: 35m

NUTRITION FACTS

Calories: 190.8 | Carbohydrates: 8.5g | Protein: 24g | Cholesterol: 172.5mg | Sodium: 175.1mg

INGREDIENTS

- 1 teaspoon Vegetable oil, canola
- 1/2cup Onions, raw
- 1/2cup Peppers, sweet, red, raw; red bell pepper
- 1 clove Garlic, raw
- 1 teaspoon cumin, ground
- 3/4 teaspoon Spices, coriander seed
- 1/2teaspoon Spices, curry powder
- 1/2 cup light coconut milk
- 1 teaspoon Sugars, granulated
- 1/4 teaspoon dried red pepper flakes
- 1 pound Shrimp, fresh, raw, jumbo (11-15)
- 1 tablespoon Cornstarch
- 1 tablespoon Water, municipal
- 2 tablespoons Cilantro, raw

DIRECTIONS

1. Heat oil in large, nonstick saucepan over medium heat. Saute onion, red pepper, and garlic until vegetables begin to soften, about 3 minutes.
2. Season with cumin, coriander, and curry powder. Cook for 1 more minute. Stir in coconut milk, sugar, and crushed red pepper flakes. Bring to a boil. Reduce heat, and simmer, uncovered for 2 minutes.
3. Stir in shrimp, and increase heat to medium-high. Cook and stir until shrimp is cooked through, about 4 minutes.
4. In a small bowl, combine cornstarch with 1 tablespoon water. Stir into shrimp mixture, and cook until sauce has thickened, about 1 minute. Stir in cilantro, and remove from heat.

CAJUN SHRIMP ORECCHIETTE

Servings: 6 | Prep: 15m | Cooks: 20m | Total: 35m

NUTRITION FACTS

Calories: 326.8 | Carbohydrates: 27.1g | Protein: 20g | Cholesterol: 142.1mg | Sodium: 313.4mg

INGREDIENTS

- 2 cups orecchiette pasta, dry
- 1/3 cup Butter, with salt
- 1/2 cup Shallots, raw
- 3 cloves Garlic, raw
- 1/4 cup Onions, spring or scallions (includes tops and bulb), raw
- 1 1/2 teaspoons Cajun Seasoning LF
- 1 teaspoon Spices, pepper, black
- 1 cup Alcoholic beverage, wine, table, white
- 1 cup roma (plum) tomato
- 1 pound Crustaceans, shrimp, mixed species, raw
- 1 cup baby spinach

DIRECTIONS

1. Bring a large pot of lightly salted water to a boil. Add orecchiette pasta, and cook for 9 to 11 minutes, until almost al dente; drain.
2. Melt butter in a medium skillet over medium heat. Stir in shallots, garlic, and green onion. Season with Cajun seasoning and pepper, and cook about 2 minutes. Mix in wine, tomatoes, and shrimp. Continue to cook and stir until shrimp are opaque. Mix in the pasta and spinach, cover, and simmer 3 to 5 minutes, until pasta is al dente and spinach has wilted.

SPICY SHRIMP AND GRITS

Servings: 8 | Prep: 25m | Cooks: 1h | Total: 1h25m

NUTRITION FACTS

Calories: 280.7 | Carbohydrates: 20.2g | Protein: 19.7g | Cholesterol: 117.1mg | Sodium: 749.5mg

INGREDIENTS

- 4 cups Swanson Clear Chicken Broth CAM
- 1 teaspoon Salt, table
- 1 cup Cereals, corn grits, white, regular, quick, enriched, dry, (corn)
- 2 tablespoons Margarine, regular, hard, corn (hydrogenated and regular)
- 1 bunch Onions, spring or scallions (includes tops and bulb), raw
- 1 Peppers, sweet, green, raw; green bell pepper
- 2 cloves Garlic, raw
- 1 pound Shrimp, fresh, raw, small (36-45)
- 1 cup Cheese, monterey
- 3/4 cup Cheese, Cheddar, sharp
- 1 (10 ounce) can Tomatoes, red, ripe, canned, with green chilies
- 1/2 teaspoon Spices, pepper, black
- 1/4 cup Cheese, Cheddar, sharp

DIRECTIONS

1. Preheat oven to 350 degrees F (175 degrees C). Grease a 9x12 inch baking dish.
2. Bring chicken broth and salt to a boil in a large saucepan over high heat. Stir in the grits, return to a simmer, then reduce heat to medium-low, and continue cooking for 20 minutes, stirring frequently.
3. Meanwhile, melt the margarine in a skillet over medium heat. Stir in the green onions, green pepper, and garlic; cook until the peppers have softened, about 5 minutes. Stir in the shrimp, and cook until they begin to firm.
4. Stir the Monterey Jack cheese, 3/4 cup Cheddar cheese, shrimp and vegetable mixture, canned tomatoes, and black pepper into the grits; pour into prepared baking dish and sprinkle with remaining 1/4 cup Cheddar cheese.
5. Bake in preheated oven until the cheese is bubbly and beginning to brown, 30 to 45 minutes.

FRIED BUTTERFLIED SHRIMP

Servings: 4 | Prep: 25m | Cooks: 10m | Total: 35m

NUTRITION FACTS

Calories: 795.3 | Carbohydrates: 83.9g | Protein: 33.5g | Cholesterol: 265.5mg | Sodium: 609.7mg

INGREDIENTS

- 1 pound Crustaceans, shrimp, mixed species, raw
- 1 quart Water, municipal
- 1 1/2 cups Cornstarch
- 2 Egg, whole, raw, fresh
- 2 cups Bread crumbs, dry, grated, plain
- 5 cups oil for frying

DIRECTIONS

1. Preheat deep fryer or skillet with oil to 350 degrees F (175 degrees C).
2. In a large bowl, pour in water and mix in cornstarch and eggs.
3. Dip the shrimp into the mixture allowing them to be completely coated. Then roll the shrimp in the breadcrumbs. Coat the shrimp well with the breadcrumbs. Mix up the cornstarch batter again. Dip the breadcrumbs coated shrimp back into the cornstarch batter. Roll the shrimp in the breadcrumbs for a second time. Repeat for each shrimp.
4. Drop shrimp, one at a time, into the hot oil and cook shrimp until they are golden brown.

LEMONY SHRIMP OVER BROWN RICE

Servings: 4 | Prep: 15m | Cooks: 20m | Total: 35m

NUTRITION FACTS

Calories: 550.6 | Carbohydrates: 40.2g | Protein: 38.5g | Cholesterol: 281.7mg | Sodium: 322.4mg

INGREDIENTS

- 1 cup Rice, brown, medium-grain, raw
- 1 2/3 cups Water, municipal
- 3 tablespoons Butter, with salt
- 1/2cup Alcoholic beverage, wine, table, white
- 2 tablespoons Lemon juice, raw
- 1 1/2pounds Shrimp, fresh, raw, medium (31-35)

- 3 tablespoons Oil, olive, salad or cooking
- 2 cloves Garlic, raw
- 1/4 cup Italian flat leaf parsley
- 1/2 teaspoon Cornstarch

DIRECTIONS

1. Combine the brown rice and water in a small saucepan. Bring to a boil, reduce heat to low and cook until all the water is absorbed, about 25 minutes.
2. Melt the butter with the olive oil in a skillet over medium heat; cook the garlic in the butter and oil until fragrant, 1 to 2 minutes. Pour in the wine and lemon juice; reduce heat to medium-low and simmer. Stir in the shrimp and cook until the shrimp turns pink, stirring regularly, 5 to 7 minutes. Sprinkle the parsley over the shrimp and cook another 2 minutes. Add the cornstarch to the liquid and stir until it thickens, about 1 minute more. Serve hot over the brown rice.

SEXY SHRIMP SCAMPI

Servings: 2 | Prep: 20m | Cooks: 15m | Total: 45m

NUTRITION FACTS

Calories: 342 | Carbohydrates: 1.2g | Fat: 26.3g | Protein: 24.8g | Cholesterol: 259mg | Sodium: 825mg

INGREDIENTS

- 30 medium shrimp - peeled and deveined
- 2 tablespoons olive oil
- 2 tablespoons butter, melted
- 2 cloves garlic, minced
- 1/2 teaspoon kosher salt

DIRECTIONS

1. Preheat an oven to 350 degrees F (175 degrees C).
2. Toss the shrimp in a bowl with the olive oil, melted butter, garlic, salt, and pepper; set aside for 10 minutes. Arrange the shrimp in a circular pattern in a round casserole dish.
3. Bake in the preheated oven until the shrimp are pink and cooked through, about 15 minutes.

SHRIMP BURRITOS

Servings: 6 | Prep: 25m | Cooks: 15m | Total: 40m

NUTRITION FACTS

Calories: 866.4 | Carbohydrates: 73.2g | Protein: 39.2g | Cholesterol: 159.9mg | Sodium: 2041.8mg

INGREDIENTS

- 2 tablespoons Oil, soybean, salad or cooking
- 1/2cup Onions, raw
- 3/4 cup Rice, white, long-grain, regular, raw, enriched
- 3/4teaspoon cumin, ground
- 3/4teaspoon Garlic Salt GL 0130 HS
- 1 1/2cups Swanson Clear Chicken Broth CAM
- 1/2cup S & W Ready Cut Tomatoes in Juice-Cnd-Cup SW
- 1 (16 ounce) can Refried beans, canned (includes USDA commodity)
- 3/4teaspoon Garlic Salt GL 0130 HS
- 1/2 teaspoon Spices, pepper, black
- 12 ounces Shrimp, fresh, frozen, medium (31-35)
- 2 teaspoons Garlic, raw
- 1/2cup Yogurt, plain, low fat, 12 grams protein per 8 ounce
- 1/2 cup Salad dressing, mayonnaise, soybean oil, with salt
- 2 teaspoons chipotle peppers in adobo sauce
- 6 (10 inch) flour tortilla (10 inch)
- 3 cups Cheese, cheddar
- 1/3 cup salsa

DIRECTIONS

1. Heat the vegetable oil in a saucepan over medium heat. Add the onion, and cook until tender, stirring frequently. Stir in rice, and season with cumin and 3/4 teaspoon of garlic salt. Cook and stir until the rice is lightly toasted, about 5 minutes. Pour in the chicken broth and the diced tomatoes. Bring to a boil, then cover and cook over low heat for 15 to 20 minutes, until all of the liquid has been absorbed.
2. In a small saucepan, stir together the refried beans, 3/4 teaspoon of garlic salt, and black pepper. Cook over low heat, stirring occasionally until heated through.
3. Place shrimp in a bowl, and stir in garlic until shrimp is coated. Heat a skillet over medium-high heat, and coat with cooking spray. Saute shrimp until heated through and lightly browned.
4. n a small bowl, stir together the yogurt, mayonnaise, and chipotle peppers until smooth. Refrigerate until ready to use.

5. Place about 1/4 cup of cheese onto each warm tortilla. Then place about 1/2 cup of shrimp on the cheese. Top with 1/4 cup of beans, and 1/4 cup of rice. Spread on about a tablespoon of the chipotle sauce, and salsa to taste. Roll up, and serve.

QUICK AND EASY SHRIMP SCAMPI

Servings: 4 | Prep: 5m | Cooks: 25m | Total: 30m

NUTRITION FACTS

Calories: 892 | Carbohydrates: 108g | Protein: 42.5g | Cholesterol: 203mg | Sodium: 456.2mg

INGREDIENTS

- 1 pound GG Linguine Pasta Semolina-Dry-5/8"Crcl QK
- 1/4 cup Butter, with salt
- 5 cloves Garlic, raw
- 1 pound Crustaceans, shrimp, mixed species, raw
- 1 cup Bread crumbs, dry, grated, plain
- 1/2 cup Alcoholic beverage, wine, table, white
- 1 Lemons, raw, with peel
- 1/4 cup olive oil, extra light

DIRECTIONS

1. Preheat oven to 350 degrees F (175 degrees C).
2. Bring a large pot of salted water to a boil, add pasta, and cook until al dente. Drain pasta, and set aside.
3. In a large skillet, melt butter over medium heat. Add most of the garlic, keeping some for later. Coat the garlic completely with butter. Do not let the garlic brown. Add shrimp, and toss to coat. Immediately remove pan from heat; shrimp will not be cooked yet.
4. Sprinkle the shrimp with breadcrumbs (enough to coat the shrimp), and transfer the entire mixture to a medium casserole dish. Pour wine and the lemon juice over the shrimp. Cover, and bake at 350 degrees F (175 degrees C) for 10 minutes.
5. Remove cover, and bake an additional 5 minutes.
6. In a small saucepan heat olive oil with remaining garlic. Toss the pasta with the olive oil and garlic mixture. Serve the shrimp over the pasta with additional lemon slices on the side.

BRANDIED SHRIMP WITH PASTA

Servings: 6 | Prep: 15m | Cooks: 20m | Total: 35m

NUTRITION FACTS

Calories: 661.8 | Carbohydrates: 61g | Protein: 29.3g | Cholesterol: 161.6mg | Sodium: 1109.3mg

INGREDIENTS

- 1 (16 ounce) package GG Fettucine Pasta Semol-Dry-3/8"Crcl QK
- 1/4 cup Oil, olive, salad or cooking
- 1 pound Crustaceans, shrimp, mixed species, raw
- 6 Onions, spring or scallions (includes tops and bulb), raw
- 4 cloves Garlic, raw
- 1/4 cup brandy, 100 proof
- 2 large Tomatoes, red, ripe, raw
- 1/2cup Alcoholic beverage, wine, table, white
- 1/2cup Butter, with salt
- 1/2cup Basil, fresh
- 2 teaspoons Salt, table
- 1 teaspoon Spices, pepper, black
- 1/2 cup Cheese, parmesan, grated

DIRECTIONS

1. Bring a large pot of lightly salted water to a boil. Add pasta and cook for 8 to 10 minutes or until al dente; drain.
2. Heat olive oil in a large skillet over medium heat. Saute shrimp until pink. Stir in green onions, garlic and brandy. Carefully ignite brandy with a match, or the gas flame. Cook for 2 minutes. Add chopped tomatoes, and cook 2 minutes. Stir in wine and butter, and season with basil, salt and pepper. Cook for 3 minutes. Stir in Parmesan. Toss with pasta until evenly coated.

SEAFOOD CIOPPINO

Servings: 8 | Prep: 30m | Cooks: 2h15m | Total: 2h45m

NUTRITION FACTS

Calories: 303.1 | Carbohydrates: 16.5g | Protein: 34.3g | Cholesterol: 98.2mg | Sodium: 563.7mg

INGREDIENTS

- 1/4 cup Oil, olive, salad or cooking
- 1 Onions, raw
- 4 cloves Garlic, raw
- 1 Peppers, sweet, green, raw; green bell pepper
- 1 Peppers, hot chile, red, raw
- 1/2 cup Parsley, raw
- 1/4teaspoon Salt, table
- 2 teaspoons Spices, basil, ground
- 1 teaspoon Spices, oregano, ground
- 1 teaspoon Spices, thyme, dried
- 1 (28 ounce) can Tomatoes, crushed, canned
- 1 (8 ounce) can Tomato products, canned, sauce
- 1/2 cup Water, municipal
- 1 pinch Spices, paprika
- 1 pinch Spices, pepper, red or cayenne
- 1 cup Alcoholic beverage, wine, table, white
- 1 (10 ounce) can Mollusks, clam, mixed species, canned, drained solids
- 25 Mollusks, mussel, blue, raw
- 25 Crustaceans, shrimp, mixed species, raw
- 10 ounces sea scallops, raw
- 1 pound Finfish, cod, Atlantic, raw

DIRECTIONS

1. In a large pot over medium heat, heat the olive oil, and saute the onion, garlic, bell pepper, and chile pepper until tender. Add parsley, salt and pepper, basil, oregano, thyme, tomatoes, tomato sauce, water, paprika, cayenne pepper, and juice from the clams. Stir well, reduce heat, and simmer 1 to 2 hours, adding wine a little at a time.
2. About 10 minutes before serving, add clams, mussels, prawns, scallops, and cod. Turn the heat up slightly and stir. When the seafood is cooked through (the mussels will have opened, the prawns turned pink, and the cod will be flaky) serve your delicious cioppino.

STUFFED EGGPLANT WITH SHRIMP AND BASIL

Servings: 2 | Prep: 30m | Cooks: 45m | Total: 1h15m

NUTRITION FACTS

Calories: 923.9 | Carbohydrates: 59.1g | Protein: 22.6g | Cholesterol: 53.7mg | Sodium: 2380.3mg

INGREDIENTS

- 1 Eggplant, raw
- 1/2cup Oil, olive, salad or cooking
- 1 teaspoon Salt, table
- 8 Crustaceans, shrimp, mixed species, raw
- 1/8 cup Basil, fresh
- 2 cloves Garlic, raw
- 1/2cup Alcoholic beverage, wine, table, white
- 1 cup Progresso Italian Style Bread Crumbs PLB
- 1/2 cup Cheese, parmesan, grated

DIRECTIONS

1. Preheat oven to 350 degrees F (175 degrees C). Scoop out the flesh of the eggplant, chop, and reserve. Coat shells with olive oil, and season with salt and pepper; set aside.
2. Heat 1/4 cup olive oil in a large, deep skillet over medium high heat. Saute shrimp, basil and garlic until shrimp turns pink, about 1 minute. Stir in the reserved chopped eggplant. Season with salt and pepper. Pour in wine, and cook 5 minutes.
3. Transfer to a large bowl, and mix in the bread crumbs and 1/4 cup Parmesan cheese. If mixture is dry, stir in more olive oil. Stuff mixture into eggplant shells, and sprinkle top with remaining Parmesan cheese.
4. Bake in preheated oven for 30 to 40 minutes, or until eggplant is tender.

CAJUN SHRIMP

Servings: 6 | Prep: m | Cooks: m | Total: m

NUTRITION FACTS

Calories: 166.1 | Carbohydrates: 0.9g | Protein: 28g | Cholesterol: 258.9mg | Sodium: 443.2mg

INGREDIENTS

- 1 teaspoon Spices, paprika
- 3/4 teaspoon Spices, thyme, dried
- 3/4 teaspoon Spices, oregano, ground
- 1/4teaspoon Spices, garlic powder
- 1/4teaspoon Salt, table
- 1/4teaspoon Spices, pepper, black
- 1/4 teaspoon Spices, pepper, red or cayenne
- 1 1/2 pounds Shrimp, fresh, raw, large (21-30)
- 1 tablespoon Oil, soybean, salad or cooking

DIRECTIONS

1. Combine paprika, thyme, oregano, garlic powder, salt, pepper, and cayenne pepper in a sealable plastic bag; shake to mix. Add shrimp and shake to coat.
2. Heat oil in a large non-stick skillet over medium high heat. Cook and stir shrimp in hot oil until they are bright pink on the outside and the meat is no longer transparent in the center, about 4 minutes.

PAELLA

Servings: 6 | Prep: 45m | Cooks: 45m | Total: 1h30m

NUTRITION FACTS

Calories: 524.1 | Carbohydrates: 56.6g | Protein: 28.8g | Cholesterol: 106mg | Sodium: 1162.2mg

INGREDIENTS

- 4 tablespoons Oil, olive, salad or cooking
- 1 Onions, raw
- 2 cloves Garlic, raw
- 1 Peppers, sweet, red, raw; red bell pepper
- 4 ounces Chorizo, pork and beef
- 2 Chicken, broilers or fryers, breast, meat only, raw
- 1 (12 ounce) package Arborio/Arbroiro Rice-Elegant Grain-Dry FF
- 5 cups Swanson Clear Chicken Broth CAM
- 1/2cup Alcoholic beverage, wine, table, white
- 1 sprig Fresh Thyme
- 1 pinch Spices, saffron
- Salt, table
- Spices, pepper, black
- 2 Squid, raw
- 2 Tomatoes, red, ripe, raw
- 1/2 cup Peas, green, frozen, unprepared
- 12 large Crustaceans, shrimp, mixed species, raw
- 1 pound Mollusks, mussel, blue, raw
- 1/4 cup Italian flat leaf parsley
- 8 slices Lemons, raw, with peel

DIRECTIONS

1. Heat olive oil in paella pan over medium heat. Add onion, garlic and pepper; cook and stir for a few minutes. Add chorizo sausage, diced chicken, and rice; cook for 2 to 3 minutes. Stir in 3 1/2 cups stock, wine, thyme leaves, and saffron. Season with salt and pepper. Bring to the boil, and simmer for 15 minutes; stir occasionally.

2. Taste the rice, and check to see if it is cooked. If the rice is uncooked, stir in 1/2 cup more stock. Continue cooking, stirring occasionally. Stir in additional stock if necessary: use up to 2 cups additional stock, 5 cups total. Cook until rice is done.
3. Stir in squid, tomatoes, and peas. Cook for 2 minutes. Arrange prawns and mussels on top. Cover with foil, and leave for 3 to 5 minutes.
4. Remove the foil, and scatter parsley over the food. Serve in paella pan, garnished with lemon wedges.

SHRIMPLY DELICIOUS SHRIMP SALAD

Servings: 6 | Prep: 15m | Cooks: 0m | Total: 15m

NUTRITION FACTS

Calories: 312 | Carbohydrates: 4.1g | Protein: 18.6g | Cholesterol: 228.7mg | Sodium: 371.7mg

INGREDIENTS

- 1 pound Crustaceans, shrimp, mixed species, large, cooked, moist heat
- 1 cup Celery, raw
- 1 large Carrots, raw
- 1/2 cup Onions, raw
- 2 Egg, whole, cooked, hard-boiled
- 3/4 cup Salad dressing, mayonnaise, soybean oil, with salt
- 1 pinch Salt, table

DIRECTIONS

1. In a large bowl, gently toss the shrimp, celery, carrot, onion, eggs, and mayonnaise. Season with salt and pepper. Chill until ready to serve.

LEMON GINGER SHRIMP

Servings: 9 | Prep: 20m | Cooks: 6m | Total: 2h30m | Additional: 2h4m

NUTRITION FACTS

Calories: 285.7 | Carbohydrates: 3.8g | Protein: 31g | Cholesterol: 230mg | Sodium: 354.7mg

INGREDIENTS

- 3 pounds Crustaceans, shrimp, mixed species, raw
- 2 tablespoons Ginger root, raw

- 1/2 cup Oil, olive, salad or cooking
- 2 teaspoons Oil, sesame, salad or cooking
- 1/4 cup Lemon juice, raw
- 1 Onions, raw
- 2 cloves Garlic, raw
- 2 tablespoons Cilantro, raw
- 1 teaspoon Spices, paprika
- 1/2 teaspoon Salt, table
- 1/2 teaspoon Spices, pepper, black
- 9 eaches Skewers

DIRECTIONS

1. In a blender or food processor, process the olive oil, sesame oil, lemon juice, onion, garlic, ginger, cilantro, paprika, salt, and pepper until smooth. Reserve a small amount for basting. Pour the remaining mixture into a dish, add shrimp, and stir to coat. Cover, and refrigerate for 2 hours.
2. Preheat grill for medium heat. Thread shrimp onto skewers, piercing once near the tail and once near the head. Discard marinade.
3. Lightly oil grill grate. Grill shrimp for 2 to 3 minutes per side, or until opaque. Baste with reserved sauce while cooking.

EXCHANGE GANG PASTA WITH SHRIMP

Servings: 4 | Prep: 15m | Cooks: 20m | Total: 35m

NUTRITION FACTS

Calories: 512.4 | Carbohydrates: 52.8g | Protein: 31.1g | Cholesterol: 217.9mg | Sodium: 408.7mg

INGREDIENTS

- 1/2 pound Spaghetti, dry, enriched
- 4 tablespoons Butter, with salt
- 2 eaches Shallots, raw
- 1 cup Mushrooms, raw
- 1 cup Cherry Tomatoes, Each
- 2 cloves Garlic, raw
- 1 pinch Salt, table
- 1 pound Shrimp, fresh, raw, medium (31-35)
- 1/4 cup Alcoholic beverage, wine, table, white
- 2 tablespoons Lemon juice, raw
- 2 cups Spinach, raw
- 1/2 cup Cream, fluid, half and half
- 1/4 cup Cheese, parmesan, shredded

DIRECTIONS

1. Fill a large pot with lightly salted water and bring to a rolling boil over high heat. Stir in the spaghetti, and return to a boil. Cook, uncovered, stirring occasionally, until the pasta is cooked through, but still firm to the bite, about 12 minutes. Drain; toss with 2 tablespoons of the butter.
2. Melt the remaining 2 tablespoons butter in a large skillet over medium heat, and cook and stir the shallots and mushrooms until the mushrooms are tender, about 5 minutes. Stir in the grape tomatoes and garlic, season with salt and pepper, and cook and stir until tomatoes are heated through, about 3 minutes. Add the shrimp, and cook until the shrimp just begins to turn pink, stirring occasionally.
3. Stir in the white wine and lemon juice, reduce the heat to medium-low, and simmer until shrimp are opaque, about 5 minutes. Stir in the spinach; once spinach has wilted, stir in the half-and-half and Parmesan cheese. Simmer until all ingredients are heated through and the sauce is slightly thickened, about 5 minutes. Serve over the cooked spaghetti.

ALASKAN COD AND SHRIMP WITH FRESH TOMATO

Servings: 6 | Prep: 10m | Cooks: 15m | Total: 25m

NUTRITION FACTS

Calories: 165.8 | Carbohydrates: 7.6g | Protein: 21.3g | Cholesterol: 85.3mg | Sodium: 128.1mg

INGREDIENTS

- 2 tablespoons Oil, olive, salad or cooking
- 6 cloves Garlic, raw
- 5 large Tomatoes, red, ripe, raw
- 1 teaspoon Spices, oregano, ground
- 1 pound Finfish, cod, Pacific, raw
- 1/2 pound Shrimp, fresh, raw, large (21-30)
- 1 pinch Salt, table
- 1 tablespoon Spices, oregano, ground

DIRECTIONS

1. Heat the olive oil in a skillet over medium-high heat; cook and stir the garlic in the oil until golden brown, taking care not to burn the garlic. Add the tomatoes and mix well until they release their juices. Stir in 1 teaspoon oregano.
2. Place the cod and shrimp on the tomato mixture; season with salt. Cover skillet and simmer 3 minutes. Flip the cod and season again with salt and 1 tablespoon oregano; re-cover and cook another 3 minutes. Remove the cover and allow to cook until the juice evaporates slightly, 2 to 3 minutes.

SHRIMP AND PASTA SHELL SALAD

Servings: 8 | Prep: 25m | Cooks: 10m | Total: 2h35m

NUTRITION FACTS

Calories: 451 | Carbohydrates: 33.8g | Fat: 28.8g | Protein: 15.4g | Cholesterol: 99mg | Sodium: 664mg

INGREDIENTS

- 1 1/4 cups mayonnaise, or more if needed
- 2 teaspoons Dijon mustard
- 2 teaspoons ketchup
- 1/4 teaspoon Worcestershire sauce
- 1 teaspoon salt, or to taste
- 1 pinch cayenne pepper, or to taste
- 1 lemon, juiced
- 1/3 cup chopped fresh dill

- 1 (12 ounce) package small pasta shells
- 1 pound cooked, peeled, and deveined small shrimp - cut in half
- 1/2 cup finely diced red bell pepper
- 3/4 cup diced celery
- salt and ground black pepper to taste
- 1 pinch paprika, for garnish
- 3 sprigs fresh dill, or as desired

DIRECTIONS

1. Whisk 1 1/4 cup mayonnaise, Dijon mustard, ketchup, Worcestershire sauce, salt, and cayenne pepper together in a bowl; add lemon juice and 1/3 cup chopped dill. Whisk until thoroughly combined. Refrigerate.
2. Bring a pot of well-salted water to a boil and stir in pasta shells; cook until tender, 8 to 10 minutes. Drain and rinse with cold water to cool pasta slightly; drain again. Transfer to a large bowl.
3. Toss shrimp with pasta; add red bell pepper, celery, and dressing to pasta and shrimp. Mix thoroughly to coat and fill shells with dressing. Cover bowl with plastic wrap and refrigerate until chilled, 2 to 3 hours.
4. Stir salad again before serving and season to taste with more salt, black pepper, lemon juice, and cayenne pepper if desired. If salad seems a little dry, mix in a little more mayonnaise. Garnish with paprika and sprigs of dill.

NEW ORLEANS BARBEQUE SHRIMP

Servings: 4 | Prep: 10m | Cooks: 10m | Total: 20m

NUTRITION FACTS

Calories: 345.2 | Carbohydrates: 4.8g | Protein: 23.8g | Cholesterol: 233.5mg | Sodium: 375mg

INGREDIENTS

- 1 teaspoon Spices, garlic powder
- 1 teaspoon Spices, onion powder
- 1 teaspoon dried basil leaves
- 1/2 teaspoon Spices, thyme, dried
- 1/2 teaspoon Rosemary-Whole-Dried FO
- 1/4 teaspoon Spices, pepper, red or cayenne
- 1/3 teaspoon Spices, paprika
- 1/2 cup Butter, with salt
- 4 cloves Garlic, raw
- 1/4 cup Alcoholic beverage, beer, regular
- 1 tablespoon Worcestershire Sauce
- 1 pound Crustaceans, shrimp, mixed species, raw
- 1 pinch Salt, table

DIRECTIONS

1. In a small bowl, stir together the garlic powder, onion powder, basil, thyme, rosemary, cayenne pepper and paprika. Set aside.
2. Melt the butter in a large skillet over medium heat. Add garlic; cook and stir until fragrant, about 1 minute. Add the shrimp and cook for a couple of minutes. Season with the spice mixture and continue to cook and stir for a few minutes. Pour in the beer and Worcestershire sauce; simmer until shrimp is cooked through, about 1 more minute. Taste and season with salt before serving.

SZECHUAN SPICY EGGPLANT

Servings: 4 | Prep: 25m | Cooks: 20m | Total: 45m

NUTRITION FACTS

Calories: 440.5 | Carbohydrates: 61.6g | Protein: 20g | Cholesterol: 71.3mg | Sodium: 1078.8mg

INGREDIENTS

- 1 (1 1/2 pound) Eggplant, raw
- 4 tablespoons Water, municipal

- 4 tablespoons Soy sauce made from soy and wheat (shoyu)
- 1/4 cup Chicken Stock-Dry-Prepared EFC

- 1 teaspoon Ortega Red Chili Sauce/Puree NB
- 1 teaspoon Sugars, granulated

- 1/2 teaspoon Spices, pepper, black

- 2 tablespoons Sauce, oyster, ready-to-serve
- 1 tablespoon Corn Starch

- 2 cloves Garlic, raw

- 4 large Onions, spring or scallions (includes tops and bulb), raw
- 1 tablespoon Ginger root, raw
- 1/4 pound Crustaceans, shrimp, mixed species, raw
- 1/3 pound Beef, ground, lean, (approximately 21% fat), raw
- 1 tablespoon Oil, sesame, salad or cooking
- 4 cups Rice, white, long-grain, regular, cooked

DIRECTIONS

1. Remove the eggplant stem and cut into 1-inch cubes. In a medium bowl, combine the soy sauce, chicken stock, chili sauce, sugar, ground black pepper and oyster sauce. Stir together well and set aside. In a separate small bowl, combine the cornstarch and water, and set aside.
2. Coat a large, deep pan with cooking spray over high heat and allow a few minutes for it to get very hot. Saute the garlic, half of the green onions, ginger and dried shrimp, if using (see Cook's Note) for 3 to 5 minutes, stirring constantly, until they begin to brown. Stir in the ground beef or pork and cook for 3 more minutes, again stirring constantly, until browned.
3. Pour the eggplant into the pan and stir all together. Pour the reserved soy sauce mixture over all, cover the pan, reduce heat to medium low and let simmer for 15 minutes, stirring occasionally. If you're using fresh shrimp, add it during the last few minutes of cooking. Stir in the reserved cornstarch mixture and let heat until thickened. Finally, stir in the rest of the green onions and the sesame oil.
4. Serve over hot rice.

SPICY SHRIMP CREOLE

Servings: 8 | Prep: 15m | Cooks: 45m | Total: 1h

NUTRITION FACTS

Calories: 239.6 | Carbohydrates: 17.5g | Protein: 26.3g | Cholesterol: 172.5mg | Sodium: 940.3mg

INGREDIENTS

- 3 tablespoons Oil, vegetable corn, salad or cooking
- 2 cups Celery, raw
- 2 Onions, raw
- 4 cloves Garlic, raw
- 1 teaspoon Sugars, granulated
- 2 tablespoons Wheat flour, white, all-purpose, enriched, bleached
- 1 teaspoon Salt, table
- 1 teaspoon Spices, pepper, black
- 1/2 teaspoon Spices, pepper, red or cayenne
- 2 (14.5 ounce) cans Tomatoes, crushed, canned
- 1 (15 ounce) can Tomato products, canned, sauce
- 1 Spices, bay leaf, crumbled
- 1 tablespoon Sauce, ready-to-serve, pepper or hot
- 2 pounds Crustaceans, shrimp, mixed species, raw

DIRECTIONS

1. Heat oil in a Dutch oven on medium heat. Saute celery, onions, and garlic in the Dutch oven until the onions are pearly white and the celery has begun to soften.
2. Mix sugar, flour, salt, pepper and cayenne pepper into the Dutch oven. Add crushed tomatoes and tomato sauce, both pieces of bay leaf, and hot sauce. Bring the mixture to a boil, then turn the heat to low.
3. Let the mixture simmer for 30 minutes, stirring occasionally.
4. Approximately 15 minutes before serving, add shrimp to the pot and stir well. If necessary, raise the temperature to medium-low to ensure the Creole is bubbling but not burning. Scoop out the bay leaf halves before serving. Serve when the shrimp is pink and thoroughly cooked.

GARLICKY APPETIZER SHRIMP SCAMPI

Servings: 6 | Prep: 15m | Cooks: 6m | Total: 21m

NUTRITION FACTS

Calories: 302.5 | Carbohydrates: 0.9g | Protein: 25g | Cholesterol: 261mg | Sodium: 460.8mg

INGREDIENTS

- 6 tablespoons Butter, without salt
- 1/4 cup Oil, olive, salad
- 2 tablespoons Chives, raw
- 1/2 teaspoon Salt, table

or cooking

- 1 tablespoon Garlic, raw
- 1 tablespoon Shallots, raw
- 1/2 teaspoon Spices, paprika
- 2 pounds Crustaceans, shrimp, mixed species, raw

DIRECTIONS

1. Preheat grill for high heat.
2. In a large bowl, mix together softened butter, olive oil, garlic, shallots, chives, salt, pepper, and paprika; add the shrimp, and toss to coat.
3. Lightly oil grill grate. Cook the shrimp as close to the flame as possible for 2 to 3 minutes per side, or until opaque.

AUTHENTIC MEXICAN SHRIMP COCKTAIL (COCTEL DE CAMARONES ESTILO MEXICANO)

Servings: 4 | Prep: 45m | Cooks: 0m | Total: 1h45m | Additional: 1h

NUTRITION FACTS

Calories: 409.7 | Carbohydrates: 41.8g | Protein: 28.8g | Cholesterol: 221.3mg | Sodium: 2625.8mg

INGREDIENTS

- 1/3 cup Onions, raw
- 1/4 cup Lime juice, raw
- 1 pound Crustaceans, shrimp, mixed species, medium, cooked, moist heat
- 2 roma (plum) tomato
- 1 Cucumber, with peel, raw
- 1 stalk Celery, raw
- 1 Peppers, jalapeno, raw
- 2 teaspoons Salt, table
- 2 teaspoons Spices, pepper, black
- 1 1/2 cups tomato and clam juice cocktail - USE ME
- 1 cup Ketchup
- 1 bunch Cilantro, raw
- 2 tablespoons Sauce, ready-to-serve, pepper or hot
- 2 Avocados, raw, all commercial varieties

DIRECTIONS

1. Mix onion with lime juice in a small bowl and allow to stand for 10 minutes. Meanwhile, toss shrimp, roma tomatoes, cucumber, celery, jalapeno, salt, and black pepper in a bowl until thoroughly combined.
2. Whisk tomato and clam juice cocktail, ketchup, cilantro, and hot pepper sauce in a separate bowl; stir dressing into shrimp mixture. Gently fold in avocados. Cover and chill thoroughly, at least 1 hour.

SHRIMP TETRAZZINI

Servings: 4 | Prep: 10m | Cooks: 55m | Total: 1h5m

NUTRITION FACTS

Calories: 565.3 | Carbohydrates: 61.4g | Protein: 27.6g | Cholesterol: 119.8mg | Sodium: 1006.8mg

INGREDIENTS

- 2 tablespoons Butter, with salt
- 1 Onions, raw
- 8 ounces Crustaceans, shrimp, mixed species, raw
- 8 ounces Mushrooms, raw
- 1/4cup Wheat flour, white, all-purpose, enriched, bleached
- 1/4cup Salad dressing, mayonnaise, soybean oil, with salt
- 1 teaspoon Salt, table
- 2 cups Milk, reduced fat, fluid, 2% milkfat, with added vitamin A
- 1/4cup Fleischmann's Cooking Sherry II
- 1 (8 ounce) package Spaghetti, dry, enriched
- 1/4 cup Cheese, parmesan, grated

DIRECTIONS

1. Cook spaghetti in a large pot of boiling salted water until al dente. Drain well.
2. Over a medium-low heat melt butter in a medium saucepan. Add onion to melted butter and stir until onion is soft. Add shrimp and mushrooms, cook for 5 minutes stirring often. Remove shrimp mixture from saucepan, place in a medium size bowl and set aside.
3. Remove saucepan from heat. Combine flour, mayonnaise, salt, milk, and sherry in the saucepan. Mix well. Return the saucepan to the heat and cook until sauce thickens.
4. Pour sauce into the bowl containing the shrimp mixture. Add the spaghetti to the bowl and mix well.

5. Place all ingredients in a 1-1/2 quart casserole dish (baking pan). Sprinkle the parmesan cheese on top of the mixture. Bake at 350 degrees F (175 degrees C) for 30 minutes.

SHRIMP DURANGO

Servings: 6 | Prep: 5m | Cooks: 20m | Total: 25m

NUTRITION FACTS

Calories: 421.8 | Carbohydrates: 56.9g | Protein: 25.6g | Cholesterol: 130.3mg | Sodium: 160.1mg

INGREDIENTS

- 1 pound GG Fettucine Pasta Semol-Dry-3/8"Crcl QK
- 3 tablespoons Butter, with salt
- 1 pound Crustaceans, shrimp, mixed species, raw
- 1/2 cup Alcoholic beverage, wine, table, white
- 2 tablespoons Lime juice, raw
- 1/2 bunch Cilantro, raw
- 1/8 teaspoon Spices, pepper, red or cayenne
- Salt, table

DIRECTIONS

1. Bring a large pot of water to boil, add fettuccine noodles and return water to boil. Cook until noodles are al dente. Drain well.
2. Meanwhile, in a large skillet, melt butter over medium heat, add shrimp and cook about 3 minutes, until shrimp turn pink. Remove shrimp from heat and set aside.
3. Pour wine and lime juice into the skillet used to cook the shrimp. Bring the mixture to a boil. Boil until the mixture is reduced by half, about 2 minutes. Return shrimp to skillet. Add cilantro, cayenne pepper and salt and pepper. Stir to heat the mixture through, about 2 minutes. Toss with pasta and serve.

CAJUN STYLE STUFFED PEPPERS

Servings: 6 | Prep: 45m | Cooks: 15m | Total: 1h

NUTRITION FACTS

Calories: 306.8 | Carbohydrates: 39.9g | Protein: 17g | Cholesterol: 90.2mg | Sodium: 954.3mg

INGREDIENTS

- 6 large Peppers, sweet, green, raw; green bell pepper
- 3 tablespoons Oil, olive, salad or cooking
- 1 Onions, raw
- 2 cloves Garlic, raw
- 1/2 teaspoon Spices, oregano, ground
- 1 tablespoon Creole-style seasoning
- Spices, pepper, black
- 3/4 pound Crustaceans, shrimp, mixed species, raw
- 1 1/2link (raw dimensions: 4" long x 7/8" dia), cookeds andouille sausage, pork and beef, cooked
- 1 cup Rice, white, long-grain, regular, raw, enriched
- 2 1/2 cups Swanson Clear Chicken Broth CAM
- 1 (8 ounce) can Tomato products, canned, sauce
- 1 Lemons, raw, with peel
- Sauce, ready-to-serve, pepper or hot

DIRECTIONS

1. Preheat oven to 325 degrees F (165 degrees C). Grease an 8x12 inch baking dish. Bring a large pot of water to a boil. Remove tops and seeds from peppers. Blanch in boiling water 3 minutes. Drain on paper towels.
2. Heat olive oil in a large, deep skillet over medium heat. Saute onion until translucent. Stir in garlic, and season with oregano, Creole seasoning and black pepper. Stir in shrimp and sausage, and cook until shrimp turns pink, 5 minutes. Stir in rice, and cook 1 minute. Pour in chicken broth and tomato sauce. Cook until thick, 15 to 20 minutes. Fill peppers with stuffing mixture, and place in baking dish.
3. Bake in preheated oven for 15 to 20 minutes, or until heated through. Serve with lemon wedges and hot sauce.

PORK AND SHRIMP PANCIT

Servings: 8 | Prep: 20m | Cooks: 20m | Total: 40m

NUTRITION FACTS

Calories: 488 | Carbohydrates: 44.4g | Fat: 20.8g | Protein: 29.1g | Cholesterol: 119mg | Sodium: 394mg

INGREDIENTS

- 1 (6.75 ounce) package
- 1 1/2 cups chopped

rice noodles

- 5 tablespoons vegetable oil, divided
- 1 small onion, minced
- 2 cloves garlic, minced
- 1/2 teaspoon ground ginger
- 1 1/2 cups cooked small shrimp, diced

cooked pork

- 4 cups shredded bok choy
- 3 tablespoons oyster sauce
- 1/4 cup chicken broth
- 1/4 teaspoon crushed red pepper flakes
- 1 green onion, minced

DIRECTIONS

1. Soak the rice noodles in warm water for 20 minutes; drain.
2. Heat 3 tablespoons oil in a wok or large heavy skillet over medium-high heat. Saute noodles for 1 minute. Transfer to serving dish, and keep warm. Add remaining 2 tablespoons oil to skillet, and saute onion, garlic, ginger, shrimp and pork for 1 minute.
3. Stir in bok choy, oyster sauce and chicken broth. Season with pepper flakes. Cover, and cook for 1 minute, or until bok choy is wilted. Spoon over noodles, and garnish with minced green onion.

GREEK PASTA SALAD WITH SHRIMP, TOMATOES, ZUCCHINI, PEPPERS, AND FETA

Servings: 6 | Prep: 35m | Cooks: 17m | Total: 1h22m | Additional: 30m

NUTRITION FACTS

Calories: 802.3 | Carbohydrates: 65.8g | Protein: 33.6g | Cholesterol: 184.9mg | Sodium: 3397.5mg

INGREDIENTS

- 1/4 cup White Rice Vinegar CBT
- 2 tablespoons Dijon Mustard NB
- 1 large clove Garlic, raw
- 1 pinch Salt, table
- 1/8 teaspoon Spices, pepper, black

- 1 gallon Water, municipal
- 2 tablespoons Salt, table
- 1 pound GG Sea Shells Semolina Pasta-Dry-Cup QK
- 1 pound Crustaceans, shrimp, mixed species, medium, cooked, moist heat
- 8 ounces Cherry Tomatoes, Each

- 2/3 cup Extra Virgin Olive Oil NOI
- 2 medium Zucchini, raw
- 1 medium Peppers, sweet, yellow, raw; yellow bell pepper
- 2 tablespoons Oil, olive, salad or cooking
- 1 pinch Salt, table
- 3/4 cup Calamata Olives-Pitted-Each GLM
- 1 cup Cheese, feta
- 1/2 small red onion
- 2 teaspoons Spices, oregano, ground

DIRECTIONS

1. To make the vinaigrette, whisk together the rice wine vinegar, mustard, garlic, pinch of salt, and pepper; slowly pour in 2/3 cup olive oil, whisking constantly. Pour into a jar with a tight-fitting lid to transport it to the picnic.
2. Adjust oven rack to highest position and turn broiler on high. Toss zucchini and bell pepper with 2 tablespoons olive oil and salt and pepper to taste, and arrange on a large baking sheet with sides. Broil until spotty brown, 8 to 10 minutes, turning zucchini slices and pepper halves once. Set aside in a large bowl to cool, then cut into bite-sized pieces.
3. Bring 1 gallon of water and 2 tablespoons of salt to boil. Add pasta; boil using package times, until just tender. Drain thoroughly (do not rinse) and dump onto the baking sheet. Set aside to cool.
4. Put vegetables, pasta and remaining ingredients (except dressing) in the bowl or a gallon-sized zipper bag (can be refrigerated for several hours). When ready to serve, add dressing; toss to coat.

KEY WEST PENNE

Servings: 6 | Prep: 5m | Cooks: 15m | Total: 20m

NUTRITION FACTS

Calories: 910.8 | Carbohydrates: 75.8g | Protein: 49g | Cholesterol: 260.4mg | Sodium: 981.8mg

INGREDIENTS

- 1 (16 ounce) package penne pasta, dry
- 1 pound Crustaceans, shrimp, mixed species, raw
- 1 pound bay scallops, raw
- 1 (12 ounce) jar Artichoke Hearts-
- 1 (8 ounce) jar Tomatoes, sun-dried, packed in oil, drained
- 1 pint Cream, fluid, heavy whipping
- 1 cup Cheese, parmesan, grated
- 1/2 cup Calamata Olives-Pitted-Each GLM

DIRECTIONS

1. Bring a large pot of lightly salted water to a boil. Add pasta and cook for 8 to 10 minutes or until al dente; drain.
2. Heat a large heavy skillet over medium heat. Combine shrimp, scallops, artichokes and sun dried tomatoes, then cook until shrimp turn pink. Reduce heat, and stir in cream and parmesan. Toss with cooked pasta, and sprinkle olives on top.

CHARLESTON SHRIMP 'N' GRAVY

Servings: 4 | Prep: 20m | Cooks: 20m | Total: 40m

NUTRITION FACTS

Calories: 263.1 | Carbohydrates: 12.6g | Protein: 27.5g | Cholesterol: 195.7mg | Sodium: 1087.8mg

INGREDIENTS

- 3 slices Pork, cured, bacon, raw
- 1 Onions, raw
- 1 Peppers, sweet, green, raw; green bell pepper
- 2 teaspoons seasoned salt
- 1 pinch Spices, pepper, black
- 1 pinch Spices, garlic powder

- 2 tablespoons Butter, with salt
- 4 tablespoons Wheat flour, white, all-purpose, enriched, bleached
- 1 pound Shrimp, fresh, raw, large (21-30)
- 1 1/2 cups Chicken Stock-Dry-Prepared EFC
- 1 Onions, spring or scallions (includes tops and bulb), raw

DIRECTIONS

1. Place the bacon in a large skillet over medium heat. Fry until browned, then remove to paper towels to drain. Add the butter to the bacon grease. When the butter begins to sizzle, sprinkle 3 tablespoons of flour over it. Reduce the heat to medium-low, and cook for about 12 minutes, stirring frequently, until dark brown. Don't let it scorch - if it starts to, just reduce the heat.
2. When the roux reaches dark brown, increase the heat to medium-high, and add the onions and bell pepper. Cook and stir for a couple of minutes, just until softened. Meanwhile, place the shrimp in a bowl, and toss with seasoned salt, pepper, garlic powder, and remaining flour. Pour into the pan, and

stir constantly for 1 minute. Whisk in the chicken stock, and reduce the heat to low. Cook for just a few minutes to thicken the broth. Don't cook much longer, or the shrimp will become tough. Sprinkle the chopped green onion over it, and remove from the heat. Serve over fresh hot grits, rice or biscuits. Crumble the bacon slices on top.

MY SPECIAL SHRIMP SCAMPI FLORENTINE

Servings: 4 | Prep: 30m | Cooks: 10m | Total: 40m

NUTRITION FACTS

Calories: 445.5 | Carbohydrates: 5.6g | Protein: 21.5g | Cholesterol: 215.7mg | Sodium: 384mg

INGREDIENTS

- 1/3 cup Butter, with salt
- 1/3 cup Oil, olive, salad or cooking
- 2 tablespoons Pesto Sauce
- 3 cloves Garlic, raw
- 2 large Tomatoes, red, ripe, raw
- 1/4 teaspoon dried red pepper flakes
- 1 pinch Spices, pepper, black
- 1 pound Crustaceans, shrimp, mixed species, raw
- 2 cups Spinach, raw

DIRECTIONS

1. Combine the butter and the olive oil in a large skillet over medium heat. Stir in pesto, garlic, and tomatoes, and simmer until the tomatoes start to soften, about 2 minutes. Season with red pepper flakes and black pepper to taste.
2. Stir the shrimp into the sauce, and cook just until they turn pink, 3 to 5 minutes. Add the spinach, and stir until wilted, about 1 minute.

SEAFOOD LASAGNA

Servings: 12 | Prep: 30m | Cooks: 1h30m | Total: 2h

NUTRITION FACTS

Calories: 764.3 | Carbohydrates: 44.4g | Protein: 45.7g | Cholesterol: 182.7mg | Sodium: 1726mg

INGREDIENTS

- 1 (16 ounce) package GG
- 1 pound bay scallops, raw

Cut Semolina Lasagna Pasta-Dry-Cup QK

- 2 tablespoons Oil, olive, salad or cooking

- 1 clove Garlic, raw

- 1 pound Mushrooms, portobello, raw
- 2 (16 ounce) jars Di Girono Alfredo Sauce KFT
- 1 pound Crustaceans, shrimp, mixed species, raw

- 1 pound Crab, alaska king, imitation, made from surimi
- 20 ounces Cheese, ricotta, part skim milk
- 1 Egg, whole, raw, fresh

- Spices, pepper, black

- 6 cups shredded Italian cheese blend

DIRECTIONS

1. Preheat oven to 350 degrees F (175 degrees C). Bring a large pot of lightly salted water to a boil. Add pasta and cook for 8 to 10 minutes or until al dente; drain.
2. Heat oil in a large saucepan over medium heat. Sautee garlic and mushrooms until tender. Pour in 2 jars Alfredo sauce. Stir in shrimp, scallops and crabmeat. Simmer 5 to 10 minutes, or until heated through. In a medium bowl, combine ricotta cheese, egg and pepper.
3. In a 9x13 inch baking dish, layer noodles, ricotta mixture, Alfredo mixture and shredded cheese. Repeat layers until all ingredients are used, ensuring that there is shredded cheese for the top.
4. Bake uncovered in preheated oven for 45 minutes. Cover, and bake 15 minutes.

LEMONY GARLIC SHRIMP WITH PASTA

Servings: 6 | Prep: 10m | Cooks: 15m | Total: 2h25m | Additional: 2h

NUTRITION FACTS

Calories: 502.2 | Carbohydrates: 44.9g | Protein: 33.4g | Cholesterol: 250.8mg | Sodium: 11829.4mg

INGREDIENTS

- 3/4 cup Morton Kosher Salt, coarse

- 1 gallon Water, municipal

- 2 pounds Shrimp, fresh, raw, large (21-30)
- 1 (16 ounce) package Di Giorno Angel Hair Pasta-Dry KFT

- 1/3 cup Alcoholic beverage, wine, table, white

- 1/4 cup Lemon juice, raw

- 1/2 teaspoon dried red pepper flakes

- 1 teaspoon Spices, pepper, black

- 1/4 cup Butter, without salt
- 1/4 cup Oil, olive, salad or cooking
- 3 tablespoons Garlic, raw
- 1/2 cup Parsley, raw
- 1 tablespoon Lemon peel, raw

DIRECTIONS

1. Dissolve the kosher salt in 1 gallon of water in a large pot. Add the shrimp, and refrigerate 2 to 4 hours. Drain and pat shrimp dry with paper towels.
2. Fill a large pot with lightly salted water and bring to a rolling boil over high heat. Once the water is boiling, stir in the angel hair pasta, and return to a boil. Cook the pasta uncovered, stirring occasionally, until the pasta has cooked through but is still firm to the bite, 4 to 5 minutes. Drain well in a colander set in the sink.
3. Meanwhile, melt the butter and olive oil in a large skillet over medium-low heat. Stir in the garlic, and cook until softened, 3 to 4 minutes. Add the shrimp, white wine, lemon juice, and red pepper flakes. Cook and stir until the shrimp is no longer translucent in the center, about 6 minutes. Stir in the black pepper, parsley, and lemon zest before tossing with the angel hair pasta.

SHRIMP WITH LOBSTER SAUCE

Servings: 4 | Prep: 15m | Cooks: 15m | Total: 30m

NUTRITION FACTS

Calories: 307.9 | Carbohydrates: 5.2g | Protein: 25.7g | Cholesterol: 237.4mg | Sodium: 989.4mg

INGREDIENTS

- 1 1/2teaspoons Cornstarch
- 2 teaspoons Fleischmann's Cooking Sherry II
- 1 pound Shrimp, fresh, raw, medium (31-35)
- 4 tablespoons Oil, soybean, salad or cooking
- 2 cloves Garlic, raw
- 1/4pound Pork, fresh, ground, raw
- 1 cup Water, municipal
- 2 tablespoons Soy sauce made from soy and wheat (shoyu)
- 1/4teaspoon Sugars, granulated
- 1/2 teaspoon Salt, table
- 1 1/2tablespoons Cornstarch
- 1/4 cup Water, municipal
- 1 Egg, whole, raw, fresh

DIRECTIONS

1. In a medium bowl, dissolve 1 1/2 teaspoons of cornstarch in the sherry. Add shrimp to the bowl, and toss to coat.
2. Heat oil in a wok or large skillet over medium-high heat. Add shrimp, and fry until pink, 3 to 5 minutes. Remove shrimp to a plate with a slotted spoon, leaving as much oil in the pan as possible. Add garlic to the hot oil, and fry for a few seconds, then add the ground pork. Cook, stirring constantly until pork is no longer pink.
3. Combine 1 cup water, soy sauce, sugar and salt; stir into the wok with the pork. Bring to a boil, cover, reduce heat to medium, and simmer for about 2 minutes. Mix together the remaining 1 1 /2 tablespoons of cornstarch and 1/4 cup cold water. Pour into the pan with the pork, and also return shrimp to the pan. Return to a simmer, and quickly stir while drizzling in the beaten egg. Serve hot over rice.

LINGUINE WITH SCAMPI

Servings: 4 | Prep: 20m | Cooks: 15m | Total: 35m

NUTRITION FACTS

Calories: 701.3 | Carbohydrates: 63g | Protein: 30.4g | Cholesterol: 264.4mg | Sodium: 450.2mg

INGREDIENTS

- 1 (12 ounce) package GG Linguine Pasta Semolina-Dry-5/8"Crcl QK
- 3/4 cup Butter, with salt
- 1 pound Crustaceans, shrimp, mixed species, raw
- 4 cloves Garlic, raw
- 2 tablespoons Lemon juice, raw
- 3 tablespoons Parsley, raw
- Salt, table

DIRECTIONS

1. Preheat oven to 400 degrees F (200 degrees C). Place the butter or margarine in 9x13 inch glass baking dish, and place in oven until butter melts.
2. Bring a large pot of lightly salted water to a boil. Add pasta and cook for 8 to 10 minutes or until al dente. Drain, and transfer to a large serving bowl.
3. Stir the shrimp, garlic, and lemon juice into the melted butter. Return dish to oven. Bake for 3 minutes. Remove from the oven, and mix in parsley; continue baking until shrimp are opaque, about 2 minutes longer. Season with salt and pepper.
4. Spoon the shrimp and butter sauce over the linguini, and toss to coat the pasta. Serve immediately.

GARLIC CHEESE GRITS WITH SHRIMP

Servings: 4 | Prep: 20m | Cooks: 20m | Total: 40m

NUTRITION FACTS

Calories: 634.1 | Carbohydrates: 34.4g | Protein: 50.4g | Cholesterol: 341.4mg | Sodium: 1054.4mg

INGREDIENTS

- 3/4 cup Cereals, corn grits, white, regular, quick, enriched, dry, (corn)
- 6 ounces Velveeta, loaf
- 1 pinch Spices, pepper, red or cayenne
- 2 tablespoons Butter, with salt
- 2 tablespoons Oil, olive, salad or cooking
- 2 cloves Garlic, raw
- 1 Tomatoes, red, ripe, raw
- 2 pounds Crustaceans, shrimp, mixed species, raw
- 1/2 Lemons, raw, with peel
- Salt, table

DIRECTIONS

1. Cook grits according to package directions. Stir in cubed cheese and cayenne pepper. Keep warm over low heat.
2. Heat butter and oil in a large skillet over medium-high heat. Saute garlic and tomato until tomato begins to soften. Stir in shrimp and lemon juice. Saute until shrimp are pink. Season with salt to taste.
3. Spread warm grits on a serving platter and pour shrimp mixture on top.

SHRIMP TACOS

Servings: 4 | Prep: 15m | Cooks: 2m | Total: 47m | Additional: 30m

NUTRITION FACTS

Calories: 566.8 | Carbohydrates: 59.5g | Protein: 31.2g | Cholesterol: 187.5mg | Sodium: 950.7mg

INGREDIENTS

- 1 Mangos, raw
- 1 Avocados, raw, all commercial varieties
- 1/2 teaspoon Salt, table
- 2 tablespoons Lime juice, raw

- 2 eaches Tomatoes, red, ripe, raw
- 1/2 cup Cilantro, raw
- 1/4 cup red onion
- 3 cloves Garlic, raw
- 1/4 cup Butter-Honey Flavored LOL
- 1 pound Shrimp, fresh, frozen, small (36-45)
- 4 (10 inch) flour tortilla (10 inch)

DIRECTIONS

1. Toss the mango, avocado, tomatoes, cilantro, onion, garlic, salt, and lime juice together in a bowl. Cover and refrigerate for 30 minutes.
2. Melt the honey butter in a skillet over medium-high heat. Add the shrimp; cook and stir until pink and opaque, 2 to 3 minutes.
3. To serve, place a few shrimp onto a warm tortilla, top with mango salsa and fold up. Repeat with remaining ingredients.

SHERYL'S CORN AND CRAB CHOWDER

Servings: 10 | Prep: 35m | Cooks: 40m | Total: 1h15m

NUTRITION FACTS

Calories: 709.3 | Carbohydrates: 46.1g | Protein: 25.1g | Cholesterol: 240.2mg | Sodium: 1016.2mg

INGREDIENTS

- 5 slices Pork, cured, bacon, raw
- 1 tablespoon Butter oil, anhydrous (ghee)
- 3/4 cup Onions, raw
- 1/4 cup Peppers, sweet, green, raw; green bell pepper
- 1/2cup Celery, raw
- 1 1/2teaspoons Garlic, raw
- 1/4 cup Alcoholic beverage, wine, table, white
- 1 teaspoon brandy, 100 proof
- 2 teaspoons Worcestershire Sauce
- 3 cups Corn, sweet, yellow, raw
- 4 large Potatoes, raw
- 1 1/2quarts Chicken Stock-Dry-Prepared EFC
- 1/2 cup Butter, with salt
- 1/2cup Wheat flour, white, all-purpose, enriched, bleached
- 3 cups Cream, fluid, heavy whipping
- 1 cup Cream, fluid, half and half

- 1 1/2teaspoons dried basil leaves
- 1 teaspoon Spices, pepper, white
- 1/4 teaspoon Spices, pepper, red or cayenne
- 1/2teaspoon Spices, thyme, dried
- 1 pound Shrimp, fresh, raw, small (36-45)
- 1 tablespoon Creole-style seasoning
- 1 pound Crustaceans, crab, dungeness, raw

DIRECTIONS

1. Place the bacon in a large, deep skillet, and cook over medium-high heat, turning occasionally, until evenly browned, about 10 minutes. Remove the bacon, and reserve the grease. Allow the bacon to cool, then crumble, and set aside with the grease.
2. Meanwhile, heat 1 tablespoon of clarified butter in a large pot over medium heat. Stir in the onion, green pepper, celery, and garlic. Cook and stir until the onion has softened and turned translucent, about 10 minutes. Pour in the white wine and brandy, and bring to a simmer. Season with the basil, white pepper, cayenne pepper, thyme, and Worcestershire sauce. Add the corn and potatoes, then pour in the chicken stock. Bring to a boil over high heat, then reduce heat to medium-low, cover, and simmer 10 minutes.
3. While the soup is simmering, melt 1/2 cup of butter in a small saucepan over medium-low heat. Stir in the flour, and cook, stirring constantly, until the flour has turned the color of peanut butter to make a roux, about 10 minutes.
4. Stir the roux into the soup, and pour in the heavy cream, half-and-half cream, reserved bacon and grease, and shrimp. Return to a simmer over medium-high heat, and cook until the shrimp are no longer translucent in the center, the potatoes are tender, and the soup has thickened, about 15 minutes. Season to taste with Creole seasoning, and stir in the crab meat to serve.

CARIBBEAN HOLIDAY SHRIMP

Servings: 8 | Prep: 10m | Cooks: 0m | Total: 1h10m | Additional: 1h

NUTRITION FACTS

Calories: 138.4 | Carbohydrates: 2.9g | Protein: 24.1g | Cholesterol: 221.3mg | Sodium: 369mg

INGREDIENTS

- 1 tablespoon Vegetable oil, canola
- 2 tablespoons Ginger root, raw
- 2 Limes, raw
- 1/2teaspoon Sugars, granulated
- 1/2teaspoon dried red pepper flakes
- 2 pounds Crustaceans, shrimp, mixed species, cooked, moist heat

- 2 cloves Garlic, raw
- 1 tablespoon Soy sauce made from soy and wheat (shoyu)
- 1/2 cup Cilantro, raw

DIRECTIONS

1. In a large bowl combine oil, ginger, lime juice, garlic, soy sauce, sugar and red pepper; mix well. Stir in shrimp and cilantro. Cover and refrigerate 1 to 4 hours before serving. Stir occasionally while chilling.

KILLER SHRIMP SOUP

Servings: 8 | Prep: 15m | Cooks: 3h | Total: 3h15m

NUTRITION FACTS

Calories: 496.9 | Carbohydrates: 36g | Protein: 26.2g | Cholesterol: 234.8mg | Sodium: 803.8mg

INGREDIENTS

- 2 quarts Swanson Clear Chicken Broth CAM
- 2 tablespoons Rosemary-Whole-Dried FO
- 5 cloves Garlic, raw
- 1 teaspoon Spices, pepper, black
- 1 teaspoon Spices, celery seed
- 1/2 teaspoon Spices, fennel seed
- 1 cup Mollusks, clam, mixed species, canned, liquid
- 1/2 (6 ounce) can Tomato products, canned, paste, without salt added
- 1 cup Butter, with salt
- 1 cup Alcoholic beverage, wine, table, white
- 2 pounds Shrimp, fresh, raw, medium (31-35)
- 1 (1 pound) loaf French bread

DIRECTIONS

1. Pour broth into a large pot, and mix in rosemary, garlic, pepper, celery seed, fennel seed, clam juice, tomato paste, and butter. Bring to a boil, reduce heat to low, and simmer 1 hour, stirring occasionally.
2. Stir wine into the soup, and continue to simmer and occasionally stir 2 hours.
3. Just before serving, stir in shrimp. Continue cooking 3 minutes, or until shrimp are opaque. Serve with bread for soaking up all the yummy broth.

CRAIG'S COCKTAIL SAUCE

Servings: 20 | Prep: 5m | Cooks: 0m | Total: 5m

NUTRITION FACTS

Calories: 55.1 | Carbohydrates: 14.3g | Protein: 1g | Cholesterol: 0mg | Sodium: 756.9mg

INGREDIENTS

- 1 (36 ounce) bottle Ketchup
- 3 tablespoons Steak Sauce Tomato-Base
- 3 tablespoons Worcestershire Sauce
- 6 tablespoons lemon juice concentrate
- 3 tablespoons Horseradish, prepared
- 15 drops Sauce, ready-to-serve, pepper, TABASCO
- 1 teaspoon Salt, table

DIRECTIONS

1. Squeeze ketchup into a bowl. Pour in steak sauce, Worcestershire sauce, and lemon juice. Stir in horseradish, hot pepper sauce, and salt, and mix well.

SHRIMP AND OKRA GUMBO

Servings: 6 | Prep: 15m | Cooks: 2h | Total: 2h15m

NUTRITION FACTS

Calories: 393.5 | Carbohydrates: 18.1g | Protein: 34.8g | Cholesterol: 230mg | Sodium: 270.2mg

INGREDIENTS

- 2 pounds Crustaceans, shrimp, mixed species, raw
- Salt, table
- Spices, pepper, red or cayenne
- 1/2 cup Oil, olive, salad or cooking
- 2 pounds Okra, raw
- 1 tablespoon Tomato products, canned, paste,
- 1 cup Onions, raw
- 4 cloves Garlic, raw
- 1/2cup Celery, raw
- 1/2cup Peppers, sweet, green, raw; green bell pepper
- 12 cups Water, municipal
- 1/2cup Onions, spring or scallions (includes tops

with salt added   and bulb), raw

- 1 Tomatoes, red, ripe,
  raw

DIRECTIONS

1. Season the shrimp with salt, pepper and cayenne to taste and set aside. Heat the oil in a large pot over medium heat. Add the okra and saute for 30 minutes, stirring occasionally. Add the tomato paste, tomato, onion, garlic, celery and green bell pepper and saute for 15 more minutes.
2. Add the water and season to taste. Bring to a boil, reduce heat to low and simmer for 45 minutes. Add the shrimp and simmer for 20 more minutes. Finally, add the green onion to the soup and stir thoroughly.

CAMARONES AL AJILLO (GARLIC SHRIMP)

Servings: 4 | Prep: 15m | Cooks: 20m | Total: 35m

NUTRITION FACTS

Calories: 257.2 | Carbohydrates: 8.6g | Protein: 20.1g | Cholesterol: 203.1mg | Sodium: 445.3mg

INGREDIENTS

- 1 tablespoon Oil, olive, salad or cooking
- 1/4 cup Butter, with salt
- 1/2 Peppers, sweet, green, raw; green bell pepper
- 1 large Onions, raw
- 10 cloves Garlic, raw
- 1 pound Shrimp, fresh, raw, large (21-30)
- 1/2 cup Tomato products, canned, sauce
- 1 tablespoon Spices, parsley, dried
- 1/4 teaspoon dried red pepper flakes
- 1 pinch Salt, table

DIRECTIONS

1. Heat the olive oil and butter in a skillet over medium heat. Stir in the bell pepper and onion; cook and stir until the onion has softened and turned translucent, about 5 minutes. Stir in the garlic, and cook until fragrant, about 1 minute more. Add the shrimp and cook until opaque, about 2 minutes on each side. Stir in the tomato sauce, parsley, and red pepper flakes, and cook until tomato sauce is warmed through, about 5 minutes. Season with salt and pepper.

SHEET PAN SHRIMP AND SAUSAGE BAKE

Servings: 6 | Prep: 30m | Cooks: 30m | Total: 1h

NUTRITION FACTS

Calories: 332.5 | Carbohydrates: 39.2g | Protein: 18.9g | Cholesterol: 120.1mg | Sodium: 1010.2mg

INGREDIENTS

- 1 serving Pam Butter Cooking Spray-1/3Sec Spray IHF
- 1 pound Yukon Gold potatoes, raw
- 4 ears Corn, sweet, yellow, raw
- 4 tablespoons Oil, olive, salad or cooking
- 3 tablespoons Creole-style seasoning
- 1 Lemons, raw, with peel
- 1 tablespoon Garlic, raw
- 2 teaspoons Italian seasoning
- 1 teaspoon Spices, paprika
- 1/2teaspoon dried red pepper flakes
- 1 pinch Salt, table

- 1 Peppers, sweet, red, raw; red bell pepper
- 1 Peppers, sweet, yellow, raw; yellow bell pepper
- 1 Peppers, sweet, orange, raw; orange bell pepper
- 1 1/2cups Cherry Tomatoes, Each
- 1 Onions, raw
- 4 link (raw dimensions: 4" long x 7/8" dia), cookeds andouille sausage, pork and beef, cooked
- 1 Lemons, raw, with peel
- 1 pound Shrimp, fresh, raw, medium (31-35)
- 1/2 teaspoon Creole-style seasoning
- 2 tablespoons Parsley, raw
- 2 tablespoons Onions, spring or scallions (includes tops and bulb), raw

DIRECTIONS

1. Preheat the oven to 425 degrees F (220 degrees C). Spray a large sheet pan with cooking spray.
2. Place potatoes into a large pot and cover with salted water; bring to a boil. Reduce heat to medium-low and simmer until tender, 10 to 12 minutes. Add corn and boil for an additional 5 minutes. Drain. Cut corn into thirds.
3. Meanwhile, combine 3 tablespoons olive oil, 3 tablespoons Creole seasoning, juice from 1 lemon, garlic, Italian seasoning, 1/2 teaspoon paprika, red pepper flakes, salt, and pepper in a small bowl. Mix well to combine and set seasoning mixture aside.

4. Combine boiled potatoes and corn, all the bell peppers, cherry tomatoes, onion, and sausage slices in a large bowl. Add seasoning mixture and mix evenly.
5. Spread potato mixture onto a sheet pan in a single layer. Place lemon wedges evenly on all sides of the sheet pan.
6. Bake in the preheated oven for 8 minutes.
7. Meanwhile, combine shrimp, 1 tablespoon olive oil, 1/2 teaspoon paprika, and 1/2 teaspoon Creole seasoning in a bowl. Marinate for a few minutes. Add shrimp to the sheet pan with the potato mixture after 8 minutes of baking and mix to combine.
8. Return sheet pan to the oven and cook until shrimp are opaque, 6 to 8 minutes. Remove lemon wedges and garnish with parsley and green onions.

PARMESAN-CRUSTED SHRIMP SCAMPI WITH PASTA

Servings: 6 | Prep: 25m | Cooks: 20m | Total: 45m

NUTRITION FACTS

Calories: 419.2 | Carbohydrates: 33.4g | Protein: 22.6g | Cholesterol: 164.7mg | Sodium: 731.6mg

INGREDIENTS

- 2 cups Di Giorno Angel Hair Pasta-Dry KFT
- 1/2 cup Butter, with salt
- 4 cloves Garlic, raw
- 1 pound Shrimp, fresh, raw, medium (31-35)
- 1/2 cup Alcoholic beverage, wine, table, white
- 1 Lemons, raw, with peel
- 1 teaspoon dried red pepper flakes
- 3/4 cup Bread crumbs, dry, grated, seasoned
- 3/4 cup Cheese, parmesan, grated
- 2 tablespoons Parsley, raw

DIRECTIONS

1. Bring a large pot of lightly salted water to a boil. Cook angel hair pasta in the boiling water, stirring occasionally, until tender yet firm to the bite, 4 to 5 minutes. Drain and set aside.
2. Set an oven rack about 6 inches from the heat source and preheat the oven's broiler.
3. Heat 1/4 cup butter over medium heat in a large, deep skillet. Add garlic; cook and stir until fragrant. Add shrimp, white wine, and lemon juice; continue to cook and stir until shrimp is bright pink on the outside and the meat is opaque, about 5 minutes. Stir in red pepper flakes until well combined. Remove from heat and set aside.
4. Place remaining 1/4 cup butter, bread crumbs, 1/2 the Parmesan cheese, and parsley in a bowl. Stir until well combined. Set aside.

5. Place cooked pasta into shrimp scampi mixture; toss until fully coated in sauce. Add remaining Parmesan cheese and toss well. Top with bread crumb mixture.
6. Broil in the preheated oven until golden brown, 3 to 4 minutes. Serve immediately.

CAJUN CATFISH SUPREME

Servings: 6 | Prep: 30m | Cooks: 45m | Total: 2h15m | Additional: 1h

NUTRITION FACTS

Calories: 483.9 | Carbohydrates: 9.6g | Protein: 33.6g | Cholesterol: 225.4mg | Sodium: 1290.5mg

INGREDIENTS

- 1 1/2pounds Finfish, catfish, channel, farmed, raw
- 2 teaspoons Cajun Seasoning LF
- 4 tablespoons Salad dressing, mayonnaise, soybean oil, with salt
- 1/2 cup Butter, with salt
- 1 cup Mushrooms, raw
- 1/2cup Parsley, raw
- 1 cup Onions, spring or scallions (includes tops and bulb), raw
- 1 pound Crustaceans, shrimp, mixed species, raw
- 2 (10.75 ounce) cans Soup, cream of shrimp, canned, condensed

DIRECTIONS

1. Sprinkle catfish strips with blackened fish seasoning. Spread catfish with mayonnaise. Place in a shallow dish, cover, and refrigerate for 1 hour.
2. In a large skillet, heat 4 tablespoons butter until it begins to sizzle. Sear the fish strips until golden, turning once. Transfer to a 9x13 inch baking dish, and arrange fish in a single layer.
3. In the same skillet, heat remaining 4 tablespoons butter over medium heat. Cook and stir mushrooms in butter until golden. Stir in parsley, green onions, and shrimp. Reduce heat to low, and cook until shrimp are pink and tender. Stir in cream of shrimp soup, and blend well. Ladle soup mixture over fish in baking dish.
4. Bake at 375 degrees F (190 degrees C) for 30 minutes.

JAPANESE SHRIMP SAUCE

Servings: 12 | Prep: 5m | Cooks: 0m | Total: 5m

NUTRITION FACTS

Calories: 161.4 | Carbohydrates: 3.8g | Protein: 0.2g | Cholesterol: 12.1mg | Sodium: 117.8mg

INGREDIENTS

- 1 cup Salad dressing, mayonnaise, soybean oil, with salt
- 3 tablespoons Sugars, granulated
- 3 tablespoons White Rice Vinegar CBT
- 2 tablespoons Butter, with salt
- 3/4 teaspoon Spices, paprika
- 3/8 teaspoon Spices, garlic powder

DIRECTIONS

1. In a small bowl, combine mayonnaise, white sugar, rice vinegar, melted butter, paprika and garlic powder. Mix well, cover and refrigerate.

BAKED SHRIMP SCAMPI

Servings: 4 | Prep: 15m | Cooks: 20m | Total: 35m

NUTRITION FACTS

Calories: 573.8 | Carbohydrates: 13.1g | Protein: 21.5g | Cholesterol: 294.6mg | Sodium: 424.3mg

INGREDIENTS

- 1 pound Shrimp, fresh, raw, large (21-30)
- 1 cup Butter, without salt
- 1/4 cup Alcoholic beverage, wine, table, white
- 2 tablespoons Lemon juice, raw
- 2 tablespoons Spices, parsley, dried
- 1 teaspoon Spices, pepper, red or cayenne
- 2 tablespoons Garlic, raw
- 1/2 cup Progresso Italian Style Bread Crumbs PLB

DIRECTIONS

1. Place shrimp into a saucepan, cover with water to a depth of 2 inches over shrimp, and bring to a boil. Cover pan and cook until shrimp are pink, 2 to 3 minutes; drain.

2. Combine butter, white wine, lemon juice, parsley, cayenne pepper, and garlic in a 2-quart casserole dish.
3. Place casserole dish in oven and preheat oven to 350 degrees F (175 degrees C).
4. When butter is melted, lightly toss shrimp in butter mixture until coated. Sprinkle bread crumbs over shrimp.
5. Bake in the preheated oven until bread crumbs are lightly golden brown, about 15 minutes.

QUICK AND EASY PAELLA

Servings: 6 | Prep: 15m | Cooks: 55m | Total: 1h10m

NUTRITION FACTS

Calories: 476 | Carbohydrates: 46.9g | Fat: 19.3g | Protein: 26.4g | Cholesterol: 150mg | Sodium: 975mg

INGREDIENTS

- 1 pound jumbo shrimp, peeled and deveined, shells reserved
- 2 teaspoons olive oil
- 1/2 teaspoon saffron threads, or more to taste
- 2 1/4 cups chicken broth
- 1 tablespoon olive oil
- 8 ounces chorizo sausage, sliced into thin rounds
- 1/2 yellow onion, diced
- 2 cloves garlic, minced
- 1 1/3 cups Arborio rice
- 1/2 cup green peas
- 1 red bell pepper, cut into thin strips
- 1 teaspoon paprika
- 1 pinch cayenne pepper, or more to taste
- salt to taste

DIRECTIONS

1. Cook and stir reserved shrimp shells and 2 teaspoons olive oil in a saucepan over medium heat until shells are pink and fragrant, 1 to 2 minutes. Stir saffron into shells; add chicken broth, bring to a simmer, and cook until broth is a rusty brown and fragrant, about 20 minutes.
2. Strain saffron broth through a fine-mesh sieve; measure out 2 cups of broth, pour into a small saucepan, and place over low heat to keep broth hot.
3. Preheat oven to 425 degrees F (220 degrees C).
4. Heat 1 tablespoon olive oil in a large, oven-proof skillet over medium heat. Cook chorizo slices in hot oil until browned, about 2 minutes per side. Add onion to sausage; cook and stir until soft and slightly translucent, about 3 minutes. Reduce heat to medium-low.
5. Stir garlic into chorizo mixture; cook and stir until fragrant, about 1 minute. Add rice to skillet and stir to coat rice completely in oil; stir in peas.

6. Pat rice mixture evenly into the bottom of the skillet. Arrange shrimp in a single layer over the top of the rice. Lay pepper strips around and in-between shrimp; season with salt and cayenne pepper.
7. Increase heat to high. When rice begins to sizzle in the skillet, pour reserved 2 cups hot saffron broth over the shrimp; gently shake the skillet to distribute liquid.
8. Bake rice mixture in the preheated oven until rice is almost tender and still a bit wet, about 20 minutes.
9. Place skillet over medium-high and cook until rice is tender, liquid is absorbed, and rice caramelizes and crusts slightly on the bottom of the skillet, 3 to 5 minutes.

SHRIMP QUESADILLAS

Servings: 6 | Prep: 15m | Cooks: 1h | Total: 1h15m

NUTRITION FACTS

Calories: 753.1 | Carbohydrates: 67.8g | Protein: 37.9g | Cholesterol: 179.7mg | Sodium: 1788.4mg

INGREDIENTS

- 2 tablespoons Oil, soybean, salad or cooking
- 1 Onions, raw
- 1 Peppers, sweet, red, raw; red bell pepper
- 1 Peppers, sweet, green, raw; green bell pepper
- 1 teaspoon Salt, table
- 1 teaspoon cumin, ground
- 1 teaspoon Spices, chili powder
- 1 pound Shrimp, fresh, raw, medium (31-35)
- 1 Peppers, jalapeno, raw
- 1 Limes, raw
- 1 teaspoon Oil, soybean, salad or cooking
- 6 large flour tortilla (12 inch)
- 3 cups Kraft Nacho Blend Cheese w/Peppers KFT

DIRECTIONS

1. Heat 2 tablespoons vegetable oil in a large skillet over medium-high heat. Cook and stir onion, red bell pepper, and green bell pepper in the hot oil, stirring frequently, until onion is translucent and peppers are soft, 6 to 8 minutes.
2. Stir salt, cumin, and chili powder into onion and bell peppers.
3. Stir shrimp into onion and bell peppers and cook until shrimp are opaque and no longer pink in the center, 3 to 5 minutes.
4. Remove skillet from heat; stir jalapeno pepper and lime juice into shrimp mixture.
5. Heat a skillet over medium heat and brush with about 1 teaspoon vegetable oil.
6. Place a tortilla in the hot oil. Spoon about 1/6 shrimp filling and 1/2 cup Mexican cheese blend on one side of tortilla. Fold tortilla in half.

7. Cook until bottom of tortilla is lightly browned, about 5 minutes; flip and cook other side until lightly browned, 3 to 5 minutes. Repeat with remaining tortillas and filling.

STIR-FRIED SHRIMP WITH SNOW PEAS AND GINGER
Servings: 4 | Prep: 20m | Cooks: 10m | Total: 30m

NUTRITION FACTS

Calories: 203.6 | Carbohydrates: 7g | Protein: 24.7g | Cholesterol: 172.5mg | Sodium: 2172.1mg

INGREDIENTS

- 1 tablespoon Salt, table
- 2 cups Water, municipal
- 1 pound Crustaceans, shrimp, mixed species, raw
- 1/3 cup Swanson Clear Chicken Broth CAM
- 2 teaspoons Rice Wine
- 1 1/2 teaspoons Soy sauce made from soy and wheat (shoyu)
- 1 1/2 teaspoons Cornstarch
- 3/4 teaspoon Sugars, granulated
- 1/8 teaspoon Spices, pepper, white
- 1 tablespoon Oil, soybean, salad or cooking
- 2 tablespoons Garlic, raw
- 1 teaspoon Ginger root, raw
- 2 teaspoons Oil, soybean, salad or cooking
- 6 ounces Peas, edible-podded, raw
- 2 tablespoons Chives, raw
- 1/4 teaspoon Salt, table

DIRECTIONS

1. In a large bowl, stir salt into water until dissolved. Add shrimp, and set aside 5 minutes. Rinse shrimps, and dry on paper towels.
2. In a small bowl, mix together broth, rice wine, soy sauce, cornstarch, sugar, and pepper. Set aside.
3. Heat 1 tablespoon oil in a large skillet or wok over high heat. Cook shrimp, turning constantly, until pink on all sides, about 1 minute. Stir in garlic, ginger, and 2 teaspoons oil. Stir in snow peas, chives, and 1/4 teaspoon salt; stir-fry 1 minute more.
4. Stir broth mixture into skillet, and continue cooking until sauce thickens. Serve immediately.

MERWIN'S SHRIMP GUMBO

Servings: 8 | Prep: 30m | Cooks: 2h15m | Total: 2h45m

NUTRITION FACTS

Calories: 836.9 | Carbohydrates: 19.1g | Protein: 69g | Cholesterol: 327.7mg | Sodium: 822.6mg

INGREDIENTS

- 1 pound Smoked link sausage, pork and beef
- 1/2 cup Oil, vegetable corn, salad or cooking
- 1 (4 pound) whole chicken, bone in
- 2/3 cup Wheat flour, white, all-purpose, enriched, bleached
- 2 cups Onions, raw
- 1/2 cup Onions, spring or scallions (includes tops and bulb), raw
- 2/3 cup Peppers, sweet, green, raw; green bell pepper
- 2 tablespoons Parsley, raw
- 1 tablespoon Garlic, raw
- 2 pounds Crustaceans, shrimp, mixed species, raw
- 8 cups Water, municipal
- Salt, table
- Spices, pepper, black
- 1/8 teaspoon Spices, pepper, red or cayenne
- 1 teaspoon Spices, thyme, dried
- 2 Spices, bay leaf, crumbled
- file powder (powdered sassafras leaves)

DIRECTIONS

1. In a medium skillet, brown the sausage over medium heat. Remove from pan, and drain on paper towels to remove some of the fat. Discard fat in pan.
2. In a large skillet, heat vegetable oil over high heat. Brown chicken pieces in hot oil. Turn frequently until golden brown on all sides. Transfer chicken to a dish, leaving oil in pan. Set chicken aside, but keep warm.
3. Make a roux by whisking flour into the hot vegetable oil. Turn heat down to low. Continue cooking flour and oil mixture, stirring constantly, until it reaches a dark brown color. This may take 30 to 45 minutes; the darker the roux, the better the final gumbo.
4. When the roux is a dark brown color, quickly add the sausage, onion, green onion tops, green pepper, parsley, and garlic. Cook over low heat until the vegetables are wilted, about 10 minutes, stirring constantly.

5. Stir in 2 cups water and spices. Add chicken parts. Add rest of the water slowly. Bring mixture to a boil, and reduce heat. Simmer for about 45 minutes, until chicken is done and tender.

6. Remove chicken pieces, and save for another use. Add shrimp to gumbo; cook for about 8 to 10 minutes more. Remove bay leaves. Taste, and adjust seasoning. Serve gumbo in deep bowls. Sprinkle file powder over individual servings, and stir in.

THAI NOODLE SALAD

Servings: 20 | Prep: 1h | Cooks: 15m | Total: 1h15m

NUTRITION FACTS

Calories: 140.7 | Carbohydrates: 16.4g | Protein: 7.6g | Cholesterol: 22.7mg | Sodium: 472.8mg

INGREDIENTS

- 1 (12 ounce) package Di Giorno Angel Hair Pasta-Dry KFT
- 3 cups Cabbage, chinese (pe-tsai), raw
- 4 large Carrots, raw
- 1 small Peppers, sweet, green, raw; green bell pepper
- 1 small Peppers, sweet, red, raw; red bell pepper
- 1 small Peppers, sweet, yellow, raw; yellow bell pepper
- 1 bunch Cilantro, raw
- 1 bunch Onions, spring or scallions (includes tops and bulb), raw
- 1/2 cup Peanuts, all types, dry-roasted, without salt
- 2 tablespoons Sesame Seeds-Whole Black AMI
- 8 ounces Shrimp-Ckd FDA
- 1/4cup Peanut butter, smooth style, with salt
- 2 tablespoons Seeds, sesame butter, tahini, from roasted and toasted kernels (most common type)
- 1/4cup White Rice Vinegar CBT
- 1/4cup sweet chili sauce
- 5 tablespoons Soy sauce made from soy and wheat (shoyu)
- 1 teaspoon Oil, sesame, salad or cooking
- 1 teaspoon Sugars, brown
- 1 teaspoon Spices, garlic powder
- 1 teaspoon Salt, table
- 1/4 cup Peanut butter, smooth style, with salt

DIRECTIONS

1. Bring a large pot of lightly salted water to a boil. Break pasta into small pieces and add to boiling water; cook for 8 to 10 minutes or until al dente; drain. In a large bowl, toss together the pasta, cabbage, carrots, green, red and yellow bell peppers, 1/2 of the cilantro, 1/2 of the onions, and shrimp.
2. In a small bowl, stir together the peanut butter, tahini, rice wine vinegar and sweet chile sauce. Season with soy sauce, sesame oil, brown sugar, garlic powder, salt and pepper. Ten minutes before serving, toss the sauce with the cabbage mixture until evenly coated. Garnish with remaining cilantro, green onions, peanuts and black sesame seeds.

TWICE-COOKED COCONUT SHRIMP

Servings: 6 | Prep: 30m | Cooks: 15m | Total: 45m

NUTRITION FACTS

Calories: 602.3 | Carbohydrates: 63.3g | Protein: 25.1g | Cholesterol: 172.5mg | Sodium: 1672.8mg

INGREDIENTS

- 1 1/2pounds Crustaceans, shrimp, mixed species, raw
- 1/2cup Wheat flour, white, all-purpose, enriched, bleached
- 1/2cup Cornstarch
- 1 tablespoon Salt, table
- 1/2tablespoon Spices, pepper, white
- 2 tablespoons Oil, vegetable corn, salad or cooking
- 1 cup Water, municipal
- 2 cups Nuts, coconut meat, dried (desiccated), sweetened, flaked, packaged
- 1 quart oil for frying
- 1/2 cup Marmalade, orange
- 1/4cup Dijon Mustard NB
- 1/4cup Honey, strained or extracted
- 1/4 teaspoon Sauce, ready-to-serve, pepper or hot

DIRECTIONS

1. Peel, devein and wash shrimp. Dry well on paper towels.
2. Mix together flour, cornstarch, salt and white pepper. Add 2 tablespoons of vegetable oil and the ice water. Stir to blend.

3. Pour the coconut into a shallow pan. Dip the shrimp one at a time into the batter, then roll the shrimp in the coconut. Once coated, place each shrimp into a frying pan of oil heated to 350 degrees F (175 degrees C). Fry the shrimp in the hot oil until lightly browned; about 4 minutes.
4. Bake the fried shrimp in a preheated 300 degrees F (150 degrees C) oven for 5 minutes.
5. Make the dipping sauce: combine marmalade, mustard, honey and hot sauce in a small bowl. Mix well. Serve the shrimp and dipping sauce side by side.

SHRIMP SALSA

Servings: 12 | Prep: 20m | Cooks: 0m | Total: 1h20m | Additional: 1h

NUTRITION FACTS

Calories: 26.1 | Carbohydrates: 1.7g | Protein: 4.1g | Cholesterol: 28.8mg | Sodium: 223.1mg

INGREDIENTS

- 1/2 pound Shrimp, fresh, frozen, small (36-45)
- 2 roma (plum) tomato
- 1/2 red onion
- 1/4 cup Cilantro, raw
- 1/4 cup Lime juice, raw
- 1 teaspoon Salt, table
- 1 teaspoon Spices, pepper, black
- 1 clove Garlic, raw

DIRECTIONS

1. Stir the salad shrimp, tomatoes, onion, cilantro, lime juice, salt, pepper, and garlic together in a large glass bowl. Cover with plastic wrap and refrigerate until the flavors combine, at least 1 hour. Serve cold.

AMAZING CRAB SHELLS

Servings: 36 | Prep: 2h40m | Cooks: 0m | Total: 2h40m

NUTRITION FACTS

Calories: 129.8 | Carbohydrates: 15.8g | Protein: 5.4g | Cholesterol: 21.9mg | Sodium: 277.5mg

INGREDIENTS

- 36 jumbo pasta shells, dry
- 2 (8 ounce) packages Cheese, neufchatel
- 1/3 cup Salad dressing, mayonnaise, soybean oil, with salt
- 2 tablespoons Sugars, granulated

- 1 pound imitation crabmeat
- 6 ounces Crustaceans, shrimp, mixed species, cooked, moist heat
- 1 Onions, raw
- 2 stalks Celery, raw
- 1 1/2 teaspoons Salt, table
- 1/2 teaspoon Spices, pepper, black
- 1 teaspoon Lemon juice, raw

DIRECTIONS

1. Bring a large pot of salted water to boil, and add pasta shells; boil until al dente. Drain well.
2. In a large mixing bowl, combine cream cheese, crab, shrimp, onion, celery, mayonnaise, sugar, salt, pepper and lemon juice; mix well.
3. Stuff cream cheese mixture into the jumbo pasta shells. Chill for at least 2 hours before serving.

SINGAPORE NOODLES

Servings: 8 | Prep: 15m | Cooks: 15m | Total: 30m

NUTRITION FACTS

Calories: 350.7 | Carbohydrates: 46.2g | Protein: 24.2g | Cholesterol: 64.4mg | Sodium: 309.9mg

INGREDIENTS

- 1 pound GG Vermicelli Sem Pasta-Dry-11/16"Crcl QK
- 2 Chicken, broilers or fryers, breast, meat only, raw
- 2 Pork, fresh, loin, top loin (chops), boneless, separable lean only, raw
- 2 cloves Garlic, raw
- 3 tablespoons Oil, soybean, salad or cooking
- 1/2 Onions, raw
- 2 Carrots, raw
- 2 stalks Celery, raw
- 1/2 (12 ounce) package Crustaceans, shrimp, mixed species, raw
- 1 cup bean sprouts, fresh
- 2 tablespoons Soy sauce made from soy and wheat (shoyu)
- 3 tablespoons Spices, curry powder
- 1/4 cup Water, municipal

DIRECTIONS

1. Bring a large pot of lightly salted water to a boil. Add pasta and cook for 8 to 10 minutes or until al dente; drain.
2. In a deep skillet or fry pan, brown chicken, pork and garlic in the oil over medium-high heat.
3. Reduce heat to medium-low, and add the onion, carrots and water; cover and steam for 5 minutes. Stir in celery and shrimp. Cover and steam for 2 minutes.
4. Mix in the bean sprouts, curry powder and soy sauce; stir together until blended and hot, 4 to 5 minutes. Toss with noodles, and serve with the option of hot pepper sauce and soy sauce as condiments.

SEAFOOD STUFFED AVOCADOS

Servings: 2 | Prep: 15m | Cooks: 0m | Total: 15m

NUTRITION FACTS

Calories: 283.1 | Carbohydrates: 10g | Protein: 16.5g | Cholesterol: 90.7mg | Sodium: 246.4mg

INGREDIENTS

- 1/2 cup Crustaceans, crab, dungeness, cooked, moist heat
- 1/2 cup Crustaceans, shrimp, mixed species, small, cooked, moist heat
- 2 tablespoons Cucumber, peeled, raw
- 1 tablespoon Salad dressing, mayonnaise, soybean oil, with salt
- 1 teaspoon Parsley, raw
- 1 pinch Salt, table
- 1 pinch Spices, pepper, black
- 1 pinch Spices, paprika
- 1 Avocados, raw, all commercial varieties

DIRECTIONS

1. In a bowl, mix the crab, shrimp, cucumber, mayonnaise, and parsley. Season with salt, and pepper. Cover, and chill until serving.
2. Slice the avocados lengthwise, and remove the pit. Scoop out the flesh of the avocado, leaving about 1/2 inch on the peel. Spoon the seafood mixture into the hollowed centers of the avocado halves. Sprinkle the tops with paprika.

BROILED LEMON AND GARLIC TIGER PRAWNS

Servings: 6 | Prep: 10m | Cooks: 5m | Total: 15m

NUTRITION FACTS

Calories: 371.3 | Carbohydrates: 0.6g | Protein: 19.8g | Cholesterol: 256.1mg | Sodium: 454.5mg

INGREDIENTS

- 1 1/2 pounds Tiger Prawns-Raw (Philippine)
- 1 cup Butter, with salt
- 1 teaspoon Garlic, raw
- 1 1/2 tablespoons Lemon juice, raw
- 3 tablespoons Cheese, parmesan, grated

DIRECTIONS

1. Preheat oven on broiler setting. With a sharp knife, remove tails from prawns, and butterfly them from the underside. Arrange prawns on broiler pan.
2. In a small saucepan, melt butter with garlic and lemon juice. Pour 1/4 cup butter mixture in a small bowl, and brush onto prawns. Sprinkle Parmesan cheese over shrimp.
3. Place broiler pan on top rack, and broil prawns for 4 to 5 minutes, or until done. Serve with remaining butter mixture for dipping.

BEER-BOILED SHRIMP

Servings: 6 | Prep: 30m | Cooks: 10m | Total: 1h10m | Additional: 30m

NUTRITION FACTS

Calories: 1030.1 | Carbohydrates: 12.1g | Protein: 78.6g | Cholesterol: 737.8mg | Sodium: 2166.6mg

INGREDIENTS

- 1 pound Butter, with salt
- 1 large Onions, raw
- 1 tablespoon Salt, table
- 5 pounds Shrimp, fresh, raw, large (21-30)
- 3 (12 fluid ounce) bottles Alcoholic beverage, beer, regular

DIRECTIONS

1. Melt the butter in a large pot over medium-high heat. Stir in the onion, and cook until transparent, about 5 minutes. Mix in the salt and shrimp. Pour the beer over the shrimp, and simmer just until the shrimp turn pink. Turn off the heat, and allow the shrimp to sit at least 1/2 hour. Serve while still warm, or refrigerate and reheat before serving.

SHRIMP LINGUINE WITH TOMATOES
Servings: 6 | Prep: 20m | Cooks: 20m | Total: 40m

NUTRITION FACTS

Calories: 458.6 | Carbohydrates: 42g | Protein: 30.1g | Cholesterol: 176.4mg | Sodium: 427.9mg

INGREDIENTS

- 1 (12 ounce) package GG Linguine Pasta Semolina-Dry-5/8"Crcl QK
- 1/4 pound Pork, cured, bacon, raw
- 2 tablespoons Oil, olive, salad or cooking
- 3 cloves Garlic, raw
- 2 tablespoons Fresh Oregano
- 2 tablespoons Basil, fresh
- 3 roma (plum) tomato
- 1/2 cup Onions, spring or scallions (includes tops and bulb), raw
- 1 cup Cream, fluid, half and half
- 1/4 cup Cheese, parmesan, grated
- 1/4 cup Cheese, monterey
- 1 pound Crustaceans, shrimp, mixed species, cooked, moist heat
- ¼ cup Nuts, pine nuts, pignolia, dried

DIRECTIONS

1. Bring a large pot of lightly salted water to a boil. Cook pasta in boiling water for 8 to 10 minutes, or until al dente; drain.
2. Place bacon in a large, deep skillet. Cook over medium-high heat until evenly brown. Drain, crumble, and set aside.
3. Heat olive oil in a large skillet over medium heat. Saute garlic, basil, and oregano in oil for 1 minute. Stir in tomatoes and green onions, and saute for 3 minutes. Add bacon, half and half, Parmesan cheese, and Monterey Jack cheese. Cook until cheese is just melted. Stir in shrimp, and cook until heated through, about 2 minutes.
4. Serve sauce over pasta, and sprinkle with pine nuts.

SHRIMP AND ASPARAGUS FETTUCCINE

Servings: 8 | Prep: 25m | Cooks: 25m | Total: 40m

NUTRITION FACTS

Calories: 517 | Carbohydrates: 47.5g | Protein: 22.8g | Cholesterol: 93.5mg | Sodium: 680.7mg

INGREDIENTS

- 1 bunch Asparagus, raw
- 3/4 cup Oil, olive, salad or cooking
- 6 cloves Garlic, raw
- 1 pinch Salt, table
- 1 pound GG Fettucine Pasta Semol-Dry-3/8"Crcl QK
- 2 teaspoons Oil, olive, salad or cooking
- 1 pound Shrimp, fresh, raw, medium (31-35)
- 2 tablespoons Old Bay Seasoning TM
- 1 cup Cheese, parmesan, shredded

DIRECTIONS

1. Separate the asparagus tips from the rest of the cut pieces, and set the tips aside. Heat 3/4 cup of olive oil over medium heat. Cook and stir the garlic in the hot oil until it begins to turn brown, about 5 minutes. Stir in the cut pieces of asparagus (not the tips), and season with salt and pepper. Cook and stir the asparagus until tender but still bright green, about 10 minutes, then add the asparagus tips. Cook and stir for 5 more minutes.
2. While the asparagus is cooking, fill a large pot with lightly salted water and bring to a rolling boil over high heat. Once the water is boiling, stir in the fettuccine, and return to a boil. Cook the pasta uncovered, stirring occasionally, until the pasta has cooked through, but is still firm to the bite, about 8 minutes. Drain well in a colander set in the sink, return to the pot, and drizzle 2 teaspoons of olive oil over the pasta.
3. Remove the asparagus from the skillet with a slotted spoon, leaving oil in skillet, and set the asparagus aside. Pat the shrimp dry with paper towels, and place in the hot skillet over medium-high heat. Sprinkle the shrimp with the seafood seasoning, and cook and stir the shrimp until they are pink and no longer translucent. Return the asparagus to the skillet, and cook the shrimp and asparagus until thoroughly heated, 2 to 3 more minutes.
4. Stir the shrimp and asparagus into the cooked fettuccine, and toss with shredded Parmesan cheese. The olive oil serves as the sauce, so add more as needed to generously coat the pasta, shrimp and asparagus.